PLANNING FOR THE ELDERLY

alternative community analysis techniques

EDITED BY VICTOR REGNIER AIA

VICTOR REGNIER is an Associate Professor with a joint appointment in the Department of Architecture and the Housing Research and Development Program, University of Illinois, Urbana-Champaign. He is former Laboratory Chief of the Environmental Studies Laboratory, Andrus Gerontology Center, University of Southern California, where he designed and directed the first dual degree graduate program in Urban and Regional Planning and Gerontology. A graduate of the University of Southern California with a Master of Architecture degree, Mr. Regnier is also a licensed professional architect. He has served as Past President of the Los Angeles Community Design Center as well as a National Steering Committee member of the Gerontological Society's Environments and Aging Project. He is the author of numerous professional papers and articles dealing with aging-related issues of housing, social and health service delivery, and neighborhood cognition.

This monograph is published by the
Ethel Percy Andrus Gerontology Center
University of Southern California

RICHARD H. DAVIS, Ph.D.
Director of Publications and Media Projects

©THE ETHEL PERCY ANDRUS GERONTOLOGY CENTER
1979

THE UNIVERSITY OF SOUTHERN CALIFORNIA PRESS

ISBN 0-88474-093-5

Library of Congress Card Number 79-90975

Managing Editor: Richard Bohen
Editorial Assistant: Jean Rarig

preface

The preliminary form of this manuscript was developed during a spring semester 1978 Urban and Regional Planning laboratory class focused on neighborhood impacts which various urban sub-systems impose on the older populations of two aging suburban cities in the Los Angeles metropolitan area. The goal of the investigation was the codification of simple techniques and estimation procedures for analyzing existing data and relating the results to planning interventions for the aged. The students, constrained by time and the availability of finite data sets, detailed approaches to seven different topics.

Chapter 8 is the reaction to these analyses by two Los Angeles County Area Agency on Aging planners charged with implementing the planning function. Their review provides some evidence of the gap that lies between the development of new techniques and the implementation of these processes in Area Agencies.

The project was the first phase of a three-year grant funded by the Administration on Aging and jointly granted to the Los Angeles County Area Agency on Aging and the University of Southern California, Andrus Gerontology Center, Environmental Studies Laboratory. The materials from this preliminary analysis formed neighborhood and community research questions which have been addressed in subsequent research.

The three year research project is expected to produce data describing how the resources of neighborhoods are utilized by older people in order to maintain their independence. A research monograph describing substantive products of the research efforts are planned for release in 1981.

This manuscript owes itself to many individuals. Much appreciated are the introductions and continuing support provided by Dick Lynch from the City of Glendale and Katherine Newton from the City of Pasadena. Their contacts with city officials helped to ease the burden of accessing various data sources. The cooperation of the Glendale and Pasadena Police Departments, particularly the assistance of David Aziz, Chris Haggerty, and Dent Wheeler, helped us immensely in the data gathering for Chapter 7. Barbara Boyd, Special Collections Librarian, Glendale Community Library and Joyce Pinney, Reference Librarian, Pasadena City Library were both extremely helpful in providing access to historical data and suggestions about oral history interviewees. Also to be mentioned are the numerous social and health service providers from Pasadena and Glendale who assisted us by providing information in telephone interviews.

The continuing support and assistance of Leon Harper, Los Angeles County Area Agency on Aging Director, who also wrote the foreword, has provided the translation process with clearly defined goals. Finally, the editorial assistance of Jill Sterrett and Jean Rarig and the typing and organizational skills of Claudette Culbreath are responsible for the form of the final manuscript. Each chapter required major editing revisions and reductions, for which I will take full responsibility. However, the ideas and inventive approaches used in each chapter are the result of each team member's creative approach to defining each topic.

Victor Regnier
Los Angeles
November, 1979

contents

foreword

The network of state and local agencies established in 1973 by the congressional Amendments to the Older Americans Act created a comprehensive system of supports for older persons. Serious barriers, however, have kept this network from achieving its promised goal of coordination and planning. Among the many problems that have plagued the aging network are the following: (1) appropriation of insufficient funds to match the legislative intent of service delivery; (2) prior existence of 100,000 social service agencies throughout the nation who do not share a common language and concern for coordination; and (3) the social service network's isolation from other urban subsystems, an isolation which affects quality of life issues for older persons. This handbook investigates the usefulness of various information sources for planning aging services in the community, and thus can be utilized by service planners to gain information about local systems which are currently isolated from social service assessment and planning. Chapters dealing with topics such as historical analysis, land use planning, transportation, and crime prevention all contain information which influence the social service and non-social service decisionmaking processes affecting older persons.

The understanding and use of the data analysis techniques presented here cannot guarantee that local decisions regarding transportation systems, zoning, building standards, crime prevention, and others will be made to meet the needs of older persons. However, understanding how each of these systems work is the foundation for shaping neighborhood environments that do provide supports to the aged.

In addition to the substantive value of this research (made possible by a Title IV-B Older Americans Act award from the Administration on Aging, Office of Human Development Services), this project is also notable for the collaboration between the Ethel Percy Andrus Gerontology Center, University of Southern California, and the Los Angeles County Area Agency on Aging. The effort has been a unique example of the research strategy promoted by AoA for projects conducted jointly by service agencies and research institutions. As in any marriage, there has been give and take, with the university providing sound theory and methodology and the Area Agency providing the political and administrative perspectives necessary to translate that research into products which can be implemented by aging network agencies. The contributions of both partners have been vital in overcoming the gap between theory and practice.

The model is also significant because it has provided the network agency with the opportunity to become involved in research that defines the role and position of the service provision agency. In addition, the federal funding agency has benefited from this collaboration because the results of the project have been applied to an AAA setting. The ultimate winners, though, have been the older persons served by a more effective service delivery system.

Leon Harper
Director
Los Angeles County Area Agency on Aging
November, 1979.

INTRODUCTION AND OVERVIEW

one

Victor Regnier

Victor Regnier is Associate Professor with a joint appointment in the Department of Architecture and the Housing Research and Development Program, University of Illinois at Urbana-Champaign, Urbana, Illinois.

Techniques for the analysis of small-scale urban areas and neighborhoods characteristically have been missing from technical assistance manuals prepared for the aging network (Long, 1971; Abt, 1975; Kerschner & Associates, 1973). Although such manuals detail how to collect primary data, structure program responses to mandated services, and perform simple calculations such as population projections, the wealth of secondary information readily available from local public agencies has been ignored. Many agencies have interpreted advance planning for aging services as an activity requiring either (1) the gathering of primary survey data from large numbers of community residents, or (2) the aggregation of secondary census tract level descriptive characteristics. Between these two ends of the data analysis continuum lies a wealth of data sources and investigative procedures which has not been used. A lack of variety and originality in strategies for community analysis has severely limited the quality of planning interventions.

This handbook will focus on information sources and analysis techniques which do not appear in the aging planning literature. The chapters will detail topics and methodologies that describe unique aspects of a community. The increased information that emerges through these sources and techniques may suggest more integrated, neighborhood-oriented planning interventions in an era when fewer dollars are being allocated to the planning, targeting, and coordination of human services. Each chapter will document data sources and describe analysis techniques that can be used to better understand the context of a given community.

Planning Analysis Assumptions

The following presumptions and definitions have influenced the content and thrust of each chapter:

1. *Information describing the interface between the older user and a particular subsystem has been gathered, stored, or analyzed by other agencies in the community.* Police departments, for example, may collect and aggregate crime statistics relevant to planners who are developing community service plans.

2. *Information is stored in a translatable form easily accessed for use in planning aging services. Furthermore, the cost in time and resources to make this data meaningful is minimal.* Aerial photographs and other remote-sensing data collected by various transportation and land use agencies are examples of sources that can be adapted with minimum adjustments. (Chapter 4 details how this data can be used to understand physical and geographical components of target neighborhoods.)

3. *Mastery of concepts and issues necessary for an understanding and analysis of the data can be provided to service personnel lacking backgrounds in demography, economics, architecture, or urban and regional planning.* Techniques available for predicting future population growth which utilize common secondary data sources can be mastered without difficulty. Individuals with minimal technical and analytical skills can use these techniques to predict the form of future elderly population concentrations.

4. *Finally, the data are relevant to a range of different agencies.* Understanding the interrelationships between problems may provide the Area Agency with the knowledge needed to influence other agencies whose services directly affect older people. An organization with a comprehensive knowledge of neighborhood problems and assets could easily assist and coordinate agencies and programs operating independently in various community settings. The synergism resulting from relating and coordinating independent agencies can be extremely productive.

Methodology Development

The substance and approach of each chapter has been developed through an analysis of the existing available data in two target communities, Pasadena and Glendale, California. Figure 1 locates the two communities within the 29 target areas designated by the Los Angeles County Area Agency on Aging for aging services programs. The AAA target area boundaries were defined by census tract configurations which contain high concentrations of low-income seniors.

Figure 1
Selected Target Communities

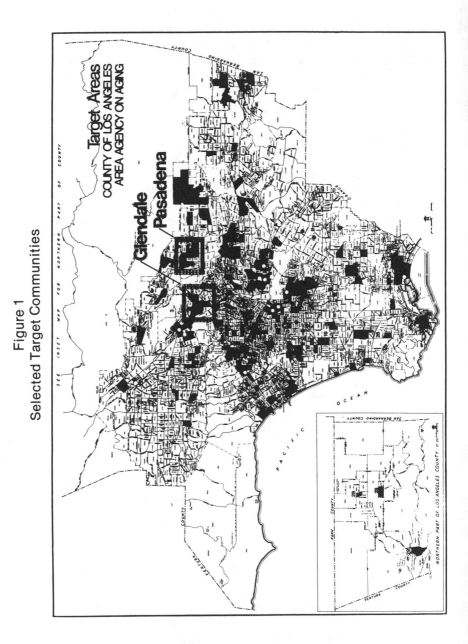

These target areas included several smaller neighborhoods; therefore, an effort was made to select a distinct smaller scale neighborhood in each target area. The census block statistics of density 62 + and distribution of home values were calculated and plotted in combination with commercial land use characteristics to identity a 200-block neighborhood.

These two target areas are similar in geography, size, and number of low-income elderly. However, with regard to ethnicity, housing stock, public service intrastructure, and crime, they are quite different. The target areas are located in separate municipalities in the adjacent cities of Pasadena and Glendale. Each city differs in the amount and quality of various collected secondary urban information. In Glendale an older section near the downtown was selected. In Pasadena a mixed ethnic and socioeconomic neighborhood north of the major retail strip was selected.

One problem encountered early in the data collection process was that certain information was aggregated at a city scale while other data was available at a neighborhood scale. Each chapter utilizes either the small 200-block area or the larger city scale as the frame for analysis. Social services and history are exclusively oriented to this larger city scale. Secondary data, crime, transportation, and land-use utilize both small and large scales in suggesting appropriate investigative methodologies.

For analysis purposes, researchers were limited to a data-gathering period of six weeks. Therefore, most of the information and the materials described in each chapter have been gathered, translated, and developed in a limited time period.

Six different topics are addressed in the following chapters: secondary data, history, land use, social services, transportation, and crime. These issues were identified as potential data sources that could be relevant to the planning of aging services. The topics of land use, historical, and crime data have been absent from techniques normally used by Area Agencies. Although transportation, demographic, and service data are currently collected by AAA's, the techniques used to classify and analyze this information are rudimentary and rarely utilize projective techniques. These chapters have been focused toward amplifying and extending current methods.

The final chapter is written from the perspective of the AAA planner. The purpose of this chapter is to translate these ideas and techniques into a policy framework with which service planners may more likely be familiar. The chapter reviews current analysis procedures utilized by service planners, commenting on the utility of the techniques described in preceding chapters.

Secondary Data

Chapter 2 deals with the information detailing characteristics of people and the environment normally available in every municipality. These data are aggregated at different scale levels and vary in quality and specificity. Secondary data sources can be helpful in making judgments about the condition of certain target areas or used as a proxy indicator of need or preference. The U.S. census is the largest source of housing and socioeconomic data available. However, health agencies, independent city surveys, Social Security, public assistance offices, housing authorities, utility companies, tax assessors, and savings and loans offices may have relevant geocoded data available for analysis.

Chapter 2 identifies potentially useful secondary data sources. Different municipalities may vary in the sophistication, amount, and retrievability of stored data; each potential source is independently described and its value or usefulness classified. Several manipulations of existing census tract information for the prediction of future population concentrations are described. Conventional service targeting relies extensively on census tract variables. Rarely, however, is this data used to document the developmental changes that occur in elderly residential concentrations over time. A historical trend analysis of elderly concentrations utilizing census tract data for a one-year period documents shifts in concentration and configuration. This analysis can be helpful in establishing a growth rate while simultaneously providing information about geographic concentrations that may develop in the future.

Data aggregated at the block group level is introduced

as a source for service targeting data. The 1980 census data will include a greater number of cross-tabulations at this aggregation level. Examples demonstrate the detail and accuracy that block group data can provide over and above census tract data. Population projection techniques that provide reasonably accurate forecasts of potential elderly population concentrations at 5, 10, or 15 year intervals are introduced. This chapter reviews several potential sources and methods that can be used to maintain updated information about the characteristics and distribution of the elderly population.

Historical Data

Chapter 3 documents the use of historical information which has been characteristically missing from most planning analyses. Historical information is particularly relevant, because the process of planning traditionally rests on forecasts of future outcomes which use the structure of present-day reality and the history of past events to predict future change. For the elderly, who have experienced and participated in a community's history, this type of analysis may have special significance. Historical events which change the texture of the community and establish social and cultural values have not been adequately related to the issues of social service provision and neighborhood change.

Chapter 3 reconstructs those links by examining the availability and usefulness of historical data to service planners. The chapter proposes three methods to gather and organize historical data. The most comprehensive technique reviewed is historical chronology. A compilation of historical events is developed from existing chronologies and a timeline created which locates events on a time continuum. The timeline can include items of major historical interest as well as milestones that have created special impacts on the aged population of a community. The timeline technique can display and classify events, utilizing any documented evidence that establishes the time and impact of a particular occurrence. The process of creating a chronology can in itself be as instructive or relevant as the final product.

Another technique that facilitates a more detailed understanding of the community utilizes community maturity patterns, which are selected characteristics displayed in graph
form describing the developmental patterns of a particular
community. Land development, city annexation, political
party affiliation, commercial and industrial land use, ethnicity
change, and family income are all maturity pattern variables
which can be plotted over a time period of 50–75 years. This
information can be helpful in understanding how significant
events have impacted the socioeconomic and physical texture
of the community.

The final technique is the oral history. This is a particularly helpful technique for validating the effect of historical
events. It can also be used to clarify or add significant historical items not documented in official historical accounts.
Published chronologies may ignore major events which reflect
negatively on a community's character. Oral histories, though
often subjective, can provide added detail. A historical analysis can be an enlightening descriptive experience that captures
the essence of the character of the people for whom the agency
must plan.

Land Use

Chapter 4 describes techniques for analyzing the effects
of the three-dimensional physical geography of the neighborhood on the development of service plans. Transportation
system design and planning service strategies are often designed with special regard to the physical layout and density
of the target area. Neighborhoods with closely spaced major
collector streets and high numbers of multifamily units
require a different service delivery approach than single-
family neighborhoods serviced by regional or subregional
shopping centers. The physical form of the city or neighborhood is very helpful in understanding how various urban
subsystems interrelate and how older people support themselves in the neighborhood.

Chapter 4 borrows from three data sources to describe
the physical context of the neighborhood. The richest source

is the aerial photograph. Aerials provide the best contextual data about an urban area. An aerial can provide information about the height of buildings, size of streets, type of housing, amount of vegetation, general level of neighborhood repair, size and configuration of commercial districts, and amount of open space. Targeting maps which are used to plot services and high concentrations of elderly populations rarely include this level of detailed information. The amount of in-depth contextual knowledge a service planner can gather from a cursory analysis of a medium scale aerial is overwhelming. This chapter discusses the use of aerials and their application to service planning. Another added benefit is that aerial photographs are often available through local agencies. Many local planning departments have reproducible drawings available at low cost.

Two planning documents helpful in understanding how the city is physically structured are zoning maps and land use maps. Zoning maps provide information about the development potential of certain sections of the city. Land use maps classify patterns of development into various categories based on the character of activities that take place on that parcel. These maps arc commonly used by urban planning departments for the development of comprehensive city plans. The windshield survey is also discussed and methods of gathering and coding salient environmental and social characteristics reviewed. The windshield survey can provide updated, in-depth information about the condition, style, and texture of the neighborhood. Aerial photography in conjunction with a windshield survey can provide a comprehensive description of a target neighborhood.

Finally, a city structuring method is introduced that can be used to establish the major environmental and social form determinants of an area. This method has been developed by urban planners and urban designers interested in how people utilize and mentally conceptualize the surrounding physical environment (Lynch, 1960). The availability of land-use data coupled with its ability to describe in detail characteristics of the surrounding physical environment make this source very useful to service planners. The design of transportation systems, the location of senior services, and a comprehensive plan for neighborhood-based coordinated services all can be enhanced by a better understanding of the physical environment.

Social Services

Chapter 5 reviews common social service inventorying and classifying procedures which planning agencies utilize to develop strategies for service delivery. Time constraints normally prevent the planner from gathering descriptive data about the type, quality, and provision of services in the community. A listing of various services by address or district typifies most needs analysis attempts. Chapter 5 develops an approach for identifying, quantifying, and evaluating the existing service base. Approaches for gathering in-depth service data are discussed, including telephone contacts, face-to-face interviews, and mail-out/mail-back questionnaires. A procedure for telephone interviews is recommended and a model instrument described. The chapter includes a description of informal services which are normally not included as part of a service network analysis. Informal services are defined and classified and their pervasiveness discussed.

A considerable amount of the chapter is devoted to the classification and analysis of various services. Salient characteristics of an organization such as funding source, agency affiliation, and date of first formal funding are collected as well as characteristics of clients. Included in this cross-tabulation of client characteristics are percent caseload of elderly, average units of service provided, age, minority status, and income level of aged recipient. An analysis of questions relating to future funding and strategies for service expansion are reviewed. The procedures discussed go beyond the traditional listing of service resources to identity critical characteristics of service organizations that affect service expansion. Used in combination with demographic measures, this service-inventorying and analysis procedure can accurately describe the many aspects of service targeting in the community.

Transportation

Chapter 6 deals with the topic of transportation, which has been given priority in the 1971 and 1973 Amendments to the Older Americans Act. The identification of access to social services and nutrition sites has been recognized as of major importance in the delivery of aging services. AoA has responded to this concern by developing handbooks that detail issues in transportation (Administration on Aging, 1975) and describe the fundamentals of demand-response system design (Institute of Public Administration, 1975). However, these transportation handbooks have been limited to a discussion of the difficulties of line haul, fixed route systems and the fundamental characteristics of smaller scale demand-response networks.

Chapter 4 investigates four transportation systems: demand-response, line haul, pedestrianism, and the automobile. The line haul system discussion outlines several evaluation procedures that can be utilized to better understand the geographic and temporal ubiquity of an existing bus system. Limitations to the line haul system are discussed along with suggestions for changes which may attract older riders. The section on demand-response systems describes some of the difficulties in creating senior-only dial-a-ride. Specific problems of dispatching, management, multiple funding sources, equipment alterations, and route planning are discussed. Critical feasibility questions are raised along with the discussion of alternative solutions.

The older pedestrian has been consistently overlooked in general circulation plans for neighborhoods and cities. Older people, because of their patterns of local service use and neighborhood identification, are more dependent on pedestrianism for the retrieval of supportive goods and services. The pedestrian element in most circulation plans is limited to major commercial strips, and the pedestrian network is rarely conceptualized as a comprehensive system. The availability of data on pedestrian/vehicular accidents as well as techniques for influencing public works decisionmakers are described.

The automobile continues to be a popular source of transportation for a large number of elderly. Automobile dependence is related to cohort and economic status (Revis, 1971). The higher incomes and auto-dependence of current preretirees (Wachs, Blanchard, Bunker, & Westfall, 1976) suggest the automobile will become even more popular as a transportation mode in the future. Driver training programs, license restrictions, and elderly-specific parking areas are discussed in detail.

A sample trip survey instrument is included to guide the transportation researcher in gathering appropriate primary data. Survey results can be particularly helpful in designing demand-response and fixed route systems. The major focus of this chapter is the development of new techniques for assessing transportation system feasibility and sensitizing the service planner to pedestrian and older driver transportation alternatives.

Crime

Chapter 7 reviews the increasing problem of crime prevention in antagonistic urban neighborhoods. Recent recognition of this problem has stimulated the development of many programs that provide training and security hardware to vulnerable urban elderly. National statistics have documented an increasing rate of crimes against all age groups. Although police departments have traditionally insulated themselves from other public service agencies, there has been an increasing move to integrate security principles in the design of buildings, specification of hardware, and the renovation of public space. Vandalism protection and the creation of surveyable public spaces are integral concepts now considered necessary in the design of contemporary public facilities.

The concern for public safety has also been reflected in the gerontological literature. Little information is available about general crime and public safety issues, not to mention the special problems of crime and the aged. Recent public opinion polls have documented the concern and fear older people have about crime (Harris & Associates, 1975), even though most empirical analyses show that older people are less likely to be victimized than the young (U.S. Congress, 1977). Crime against the elderly has become a concern of area agency planners, particularly in inner city urban neighborhoods. This concern is increasingly being shared by all individuals involved in service delivery, as victimization assistance and prevention programs become more prevalent.

Chapter 7 deals with several aspects of neighborhood crime. The increasing sophistication of police departments has been reflected in the data available describing characteristics and circumstances surrounding the victimization of older people. This information, utilized by police in investigating crime problems, can also be helpful to aging agencies in the process of developing community programs. This chapter discusses commonly available descriptive variables as they relate to characteristics of street and residential crime that would be most relevant to elderly community residents.

Environmental characteristics that encourage criminal activity are outlined. These criteria specify land use formations which can aid the street criminal in victimizing older pedestrians. Neighborhood organizing strategies such as Neighborhood Watch are discussed. Older people can play special roles in neighborhood organizations because much of their time is spent at home.

Finally, informal data collection procedures such as the police "ride-along" and the interviewing of police investigators are reviewed. The problem of crime against the elderly is of universal concern to agencies that provide community services to older people. Prevention information can be as important to the mental health and well-being of older residents as health screening can be to the identification and treatment of physical health ailments.

Conclusions

The methods outlined in each of the chapters go beyond the existing procedures utilized by most service planners for targeting services in neighborhoods with high concentrations of elderly. Better knowledge of the physical and demographic structure of the community should lead to more effective interventions. The pervasiveness of informal services, the activity patterns of elderly residents, historical/cultural influences, and expansion patterns of the elderly population can provide keys to the problem of integrating service systems. Comprehensive service planning is difficult to achieve if specific information about available services or neighborhood problems is not considered in the planning process. If the service planners can collect, analyze, and utilize this knowledge for the distribution of services, then planning can take place which anticipates problems and provides for future contingencies. The methods presented in this book do not require a great increase in data collection resources nor do they require the acquisition of sophisticated analysis skills. The methods presented are merely better ways of utilizing, assessing, and applying these information sources to the interrelated and complex problems of the elderly population.

References

Abt Associates. *A.A.A. process manuals.* Report to the Administration on Aging, Cambridge, Massachusetts, 1975.

Administration on Aging. *Transportation for the elderly: the state of the art.* Washington, D.C.: Department of Health, Education, and Welfare, 1975.

Harris & Associates. *The myth and reality of aging in America.* Washington, D.C.: The National Council on Aging, 1975.

Institute of Public Administration. *Planning handbook: Transportation services for the elderly.* Washington, D.C.: Department of Health, Education, and Welfare, 1975.

Kerschner & Associates. *How to do it handbook for integrative service programs for older people* (Vol. 1–6). Report to the Administration on Aging, Washington, D.C., 1973.

Long, N. *Information and referral services.* Publications (9) by Interstudy. Minneapolis, Minn.: Interstudy, 1971–1975.

Lynch, K. *The image of the city.* Cambridge, Mass.: Massachusetts Institute of Technology Press, 1960.

Revis, J. S. *Transportation: Background and issues.* Report presented to the White House Conference on Aging. Washington, D.C.: U.S. Government Printing Office, 1971.

U.S. Congress. Select Committee on Aging. *In search of security: A national perspective on elderly crime victimization.* Report by the Subcommittee on Housing and Consumer Interests, 95th Congress, Washington, D.C.: U.S. Government Printing Office, 1977.

Wachs, M., Blanchard, R. D., Bunker, J. B., & Westfall, M. *Determining the future mobility needs of the elderly: Development of a methodology.* Los Angeles: University of California at Los Angeles, 1976.

2

SECONDARY DATA ANALYSIS TECHNIQUES

Gerald Rioux
and Diane Oeffler Hutson

Gerald Rioux is presently operating a housing rehabilitation program for the City of Cudahy, California.

Diane Oeffler Hutson is a Research Assistant with Alternative Designs for Comprehensive Delivery Through Case Service Coordination and Advocacy, Social Policy Laboratory, Andrus Gerontology Center, University of Southern California, Los Angeles, California.

Introduction

Secondary data are available from virtually every public and private service agency in varying forms with different levels of accuracy, completeness, and availability. For purposes of this chapter, "secondary data" has been defined as collected information available in usable form from an accessible source.

The most popular and well known source of secondary data is the *U.S. Census of Population and Housing*. Although the census is a tremendous source of community data, it has its limitations. This chapter will explore other secondary data sources, and will introduce several analysis techniques that can be used to update and interpret information from secondary sources.

Available sources vary from one municipality to another. Urban areas, particularly those large enough to qualify as standard metropolitan statistical areas (SMSA), are more likely to have a broader selection of potential crosstabulations. On the other hand, information on rural areas may be available only from county or state sources. The planner's first task in using secondary data is to identify sources which provide current, usable information. Data sources available for the analysis of community trends include the *Census of Population and Housing*, public welfare departments, and vital statistics publications. A demographer and/or social research analyst familiar with your region or municipality may be helpful in establishing a list of possible data sources.

A first task will be to catalog specific types of information needed, keeping in mind the geographic scale desired. Information of high value to planners typically describes the number of elderly; social, health, and economic conditions of the elderly; and housing conditions. The geographical scale of the data can limit analysis. Small geographic areas such as census tracts are preferable for community-level planning. Once potential sources, needed data, and geographic scale are determined, the usefulness of each source can be rated by weighing the expected value of the data against the ease and cost of access. Table 1 describes the availability and usefulness of sources identified in this study. The agencies designated as "Useful" had data which were easily accessed and believed to be valuable prior to testing.

Several limitations of these data sources should be noted. First, information requested from a large bureaucracy may take weeks or even months to secure, reducing its utility if time is limited. Second, data reported for some geographic areas may not be comparable with other reporting districts. Third, information for sparsely populated small-scale districts may be unreliable because government restrictions often require suppression of this information to insure confidentiality.

Improving the State of the Art

In most areas, the *Census of Population* is the primary source of data for planning.[1] The data in these reports normally include total population 60 years of age and over, number of elderly in poverty, and number of black and Chicano elderly.

Advancing the state of the art of secondary data analysis in elderly service planning can be accomplished either by improving the quality of data utilized in the analyses or by widening the range of analytical methods used to interpret the data.

Characteristics of Secondary Data

Most public and private agencies maintain records of client activities. Such records, if in usable form, can provide a wealth of secondary data for planning. The reporting area or level of aggregation/disaggregation[2] greatly affects the usefulness of such data. Incongruity of reporting districts can complicate comparisons between data sources: for example, the Post Office uses zip codes, police departments use reporting districts, and utility companies use market areas to geocode data.

Other data requirements are accuracy, completeness, and reliability. The most universally useful data sources are the U.S. Bureau of the Census (both printed and computer

Table 1
Data Sources and Usefulness

Source	Spatial Disaggregation	Data Frequency	Data Available Elderly Specific	Data Available Nonspecific	Notes and Comments
1. U.S. Bureau of Census *Census of Population & Housing*	County City ZIP Code Census Tract Block Group Block	Dicenial (10 yrs.)	Age Sex Race Income Poverty status Tenure Household type Home value Rent Length of residency	Various	Standard planning data source. Considerable data; reliable, widely available. Various data files are underutilized (e.g., 5th Count).
A. 1) 1970 Census 4th Count Bound Volumes	Census Tract	Dicenial (10 yrs.)	Age Sex Race Poverty	Various	Standard planning data source. Very easy to obtain and use.
Summary Tape	Census Tract		75% & 125% poverty Poverty & Social Security or railroad retirement	127 population tables 200 housing tables	Fairly easy to obtain. Provides considerable additional data than bound volumes. Need programmer and access to computer and tapes.

		Unrelated individuals poverty Household arrangement Tenancy & age of home Tenancy & year moved in Tenancy & income	May be purchased from a university or various private data vendors.
2) 5th Count Summary Tape only	Block Group		
		Age Race Sex Poverty	53 tables
			Difficult to access. Rarely used, programmers claim it is poorly formatted. Provides detailed data for small area analysis. Contact Larry Carbeaugh at U.S. Census in Maryland, (301) 763-2400, if you have difficulty finding a university or vendor with tapes.
3) 3rd Count Bound Volumes	Block	% 62 +	Fairly easy to obtain. Of limited value for area-wide planning. May be helpful in targeting small area.
		% Negro Home Value, Size, Rent	
Summary Tape	Block	Age Sex	*Not* worth using for area-wide planning.
		More detailed housing data	

Table 1 (cont'd.)
Data Sources and Usefulness

Source	Spatial Disaggregation	Data Frequency	Data Available Elderly Specific	Nonspecific	Notes and Comments
B. 1960 Census Bound Volumes	Census Tract	Dicenial (10 yrs.)	Age Sex Race	Home Value Rent Education Occupation Employment	Very easy to obtain. Most libraries have current tract boundary and numbering system was adopted in 1960.
C. 1950 Census Bound Volumes	Census Tract	Dicenial (10 yrs.)	Age Sex Race	Home Value Rent Education Occupation Employment	Fairly easy to obtain. Universities and other public libraries should have. May be on microfilm. Census tract boundaries the same or similar to current boundaries for older areas. Numbering system was different.
D. 1940 Census Bound Volumes	Census Tract	Dicenial (10 yrs.)	Age Sex Race	Home Value Rent Education Occupation Employment	Fairly easy to obtain. Universities and other public libraries should have. May be on microfilm. Census tract boundaries the same or similar to current boundaries for older areas. Numbering system was different.

2. DHEW Social Security Administration	ZIP Code	Quarterly	SSI recipients Medicare	SSI—Disabled and blind	Moderately difficult to obtain. Maintained at Federal Region level. Formal request required.
3. Vital Statistics—Health	Census Tract	Monthly	Age at death	Morbidity by major category Mortality by major category	Easily obtained. Data available nationwide. Data under-reported in area of morbidity.
4. State Board of Nursing Licensure	City, street address	Continual		Number of licensed beds	Issues licenses and keep files. Does not publish data. Able to provide yearly changes. Does not keep data regarding licensed facilities rates of change at city or census tract level.
5. State Health Facilities Commission	City, street address	Annual		Health facilities Beds	Easily obtained. Data likely to vary throughout nation. Published Health Facilities Directory where PSRO gets number of beds.
6. Health Systems Agency (HSA)	Reporting District	Annual	Current pop., est. 5-year projection	Population projections	Need written request. Fairly easy to obtain. Limited value due to aggregation. Data likely to vary throughout nation.

Table 1 (cont'd.)
Data Sources and Usefulness

Source	Spatial Disaggregation	Data Frequency	Data Available Elderly Specific	Data Available Nonspecific	Notes and Comments
7. Department of Public Social Services (County Welfare)	Census Tract (in L.A. County)	Quarterly	SSI caseload Homemaker chore	AFDC caseload MediCal (Medicaid)	SSI data is not complete. Only about 75% is allocated to tracts. SSI data not divided between aged, disabled, and blind recipients. Fairly easy to obtain. May not be available nationwide.
8. Professional Standards Review Organization (PSRO)	City, street address	Annual		Health facilities Beds	Easily obtained. Data likely to vary throughout nation. Includes acute, convalescent hospitals, number of beds, type of beds, and year licensed.
9. California Department of Finance	Census Tract Block Group	By contract	Age Sex	Housing stock	Awkward to access. Data must be copied from printout in city hall. Printouts are available from DOF at cost with permission of city.
10. California Franchise Tax Board	County	Annual	Age Income Marital status Home value Property taxes		Easy to obtain. Of little value in present form. Agency will disaggregate for cost of computer run and programmer's time. High potential value.

tape material), the Social Security Administration, county welfare departments, the Department of Housing and Urban Development, and special studies conducted by local governments. Analysis of these sources is presented in the following sections.

Secondary Data Sources

U.S. Census data.[3] The U.S. Census is the standard source of planning data because it provides a large amount of useful data which is relatively accurate and accessible. Information on age, race, ethnicity, employment, occupation, income, and living arrangements of the population, as well as on types, costs, and characteristics of housing are among the data available from the Census. Most of this information is provided in printed reports and is available for states, cities, counties, census tracts, and blocks. For 1970, additional data for zip codes, congressional districts, and block groups is available from computer tapes.

The U.S. Census reporting system has been adopted by an increasing number of agencies. The main unit for Census reporting at a community level is the *census tract*. Census tracts are constructed as relatively homogeneous areas bounded by major streets, physical features, or political boundaries. They generally have populations of 3,000 to 6,000 persons. Should population increase considerably above this level, the tract is split. Major boundaries, however, remain the same to retain comparability between Censes. Tract boundaries are likely to be consistent from 1940 or earlier for older areas of cities; however, re-tracting occurs as a matter of course in rapidly growing areas.

The Census also reports information for census blocks which are generally the same as city blocks. Due to confidentiality restrictions, detailed socioeconomic data cannot be reported at the block level. Additionally, the large number of blocks in a city or metropolitan area make it difficult to use block statistics in area-wide planning. In response to the need for a spatial unit between the block and the tract, the Census began reporting information for block groups in 1970.

Block groups have populations of approximately 1,000 persons each.

The 1970 Census was released in six stages or counts. Each count provides different levels of detail for different reporting areas. Table 1 indicates relevant Census counts and lists the type of information provided. The 1970 Census provides considerably more information than earlier censes. Age, race, and sex data are available at the tract level from 1940 to the present. These data are relatively easy to obtain and use, and allow time-related comparisons of the elderly population.

The older people most in need of social services are the "frail elderly." For them, proximity to services may be a major factor in maintaining independence. Many frail older people experience physical problems that limit mobility; therefore, the location of seniors within a census tract relative to the location of supportive goods and services becomes important.

To obtain socioeconomic information within a census tract, data available at the block group level from the *1970 Census Fifth Count Summary Tapes* are especially useful. Age, sex, income, home value, and rent as well as poverty by age are available for block groups. *Fifth Count* data be used in the same manner as census tract data. Target data can be established based on percentage of elderly, poverty rates, and number of minority elderly for these smaller areas.

Analysis of block group data for the text communities showed that census tracts were much less homogeneous than expected. Even tracts with relatively low overall percentages of elderly contain concentrations of elderly in certain geographic areas. Likewise, tracts with high concentrations of older persons may have geographic areas with elderly. Figure 1 demonstrates how a tract level analysis might obscure differences between neighborhoods. These differences can be revealed by block group level analysis.

Social Security data. The Social Security Administration (SSA) is perhaps the best additional detailed source of data on the elderly. It administers OASDI (Old Age Survivors and Disability Insurance), Medicare, and SSI (Supplemental Security Income). The SSA maintains extensive records on

Figure 1
Disaggregation of Census Tract Mapping into Block Group Configurations

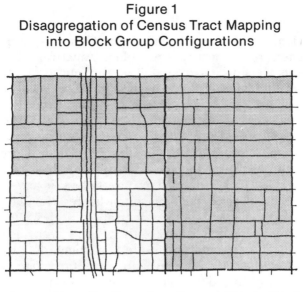

Census Tract Configurations Percent Elderly (65 +)

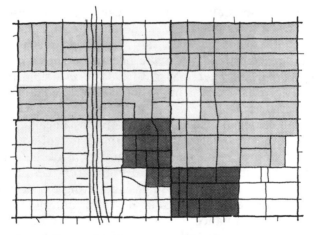

Block Group Configurations Percent Elderly (65 +)

Population 65 + (percent)

 20–30%

 10–20%

 0–10%

the location, age, income, benefits, marital status, and medical expenditures of nearly every older American. Unfortunately, this data is not available at the census tract level. At present, only quarterly Medicare and SSI caseload counts by zip code are readily available from Social Security. Since almost every person over age 65 is enrolled in the Medicare program, Medicare counts can be used as a proxy to represent the total number of persons over 65. The SSI program provides supplemental income for aged, disabled, and the blind at a rate which is defined as poverty level income. Comparing the number of older persons who receive SSI to the number of persons enrolled in Medicare provides a measure of the current economic status of the elderly in any given zip code area.[4] This secondary measure is particularly intriguing because the quarterly data available are far more current than from any other data source. Table 2 illustrates the use of the SSI/Medicare ratio for determining poverty rates.

Caution must be emphasized in using this technique. First, the rate calculated from Medicare statistics normally includes the institutionalized, while the Census does not. Second, comparisons between large zip code districts and census tracts are difficult to make because of boundary discontinuities. The planner may gather data on both zip code areas and census tracts, but should exercise caution in making comparisons.

Special censes. Because population has become an increasingly important variable in intergovernmental transfer programs such as revenue sharing, many areas of the country have conducted an updated special population census since 1970. Because the main purpose of conducting a special census is to establish a higher population count and because the community must finance the study, such updated censes often include only a population count at the census tract level. Age information and housing counts are usually included, but socioeconomic variables (race or ethnicity, education, and income) are rarely obtained.

Due to the complexity of conducting a census and the need for accuracy, the Census Bureau began contracting for special censes in 1915, and has conducted 1,341 special censes between the 1970 Census and June 30, 1977.[5] Age, sex,

Table 2

Poverty Estimates: Social Security Administration
Data, June 1977, Compared to U. S. Census Data, 1970.

ZIP Code	Medicare[1] Enrollment	SSI[1] Recipients	June 1977[1] Senior (65 +) Medicare Poverty Estimate	1970[2] Senior (60 +) Poverty Estimate
91101	2122	341	16.1%	21.3%
91103	2798	547	19.5%	21.7%
91104	4936	722	14.6%	13.2%
91105	2065	97	4.7%	7.1%
91106	3818	388	10.2%	12.5%
91107	4491	324	7.2%	12.0%
Combined	20230	2419	12.0%	14.2%

[1]*Source:* The Department of Health, Education and Welfare, Social Security Administration. The poverty estimate is Medicare enrollment/SSI recipients. The data are available quarterly and can be used to identify current conditions in the community.

[2]*Source:* United Way, 1973. Estimates of the 1970 senior (60 +) poverty based on Sixth Count Census data.

and race are available at the census tract level for those special cases conducted by the Bureau. In California, the State Department of Finance coordinates special census efforts.[6] Other states may have also conducted special censes, and should be contacted to determine which communities have been included.

Other useful data sources. Many useful data sources are available from a variety of agencies and organizations responsible for the planning of public activities. Counties and cities, health systems agencies, community action agencies, councils of governments, and utility companies all prepare reports on various aspects of their populations and services.

Directories of federally financed and subsidized housing projects published by the Department of Housing and Urban Development can be used to identify and plot the location of elderly housing in each Census Tract. The application of the data to service planning is particularly important because occupants of housing projects are known to have over-bene-fited from public services. The location of such housing facilities may be used to identify potential centers for delivering services. Alternatively, the number of elderly housing occupants may be subtracted from population counts to identify the segment of the population that is more poorly served.

The location of nursing homes can be derived from health planning agencies and state regulatory board records which list the address and size of these facilities. This information may be mapped in a similar manner by census tract, block, or block group level, and may be used for the targeting of special programs for these groups. Table 1 describes in more detail data available from these sources.

Data Analysis Techniques

Once obtained, the data can be inspected, combined, compared, mapped, graphed, and manipulated in a variety of ways. Typically, service analyses note elderly concentrations, poverty rates, and number of minority elderly by census tract. Traditionally, contiguous tracts having high percentages of all three variables are identified as target areas for service.

Three analyses requiring little or no additional effort or analytical ability deemed useful for secondary data analysis include social indicators, historical data analysis, and age-cohort analysis.

Social indicators. Social indicators are specific data items which correlate highly with certain social conditions and are commonly employed by planners of service delivery. For example, a high number of "elderly persons living alone" may indicate the need for a nutrition program.[7] Such social indicators are particularly valuable when correlated with information that is not readily available or costly to acquire.

Several social indicators have been identified and found useful in planning for the elderly. The Los Angeles City Community Analysis Bureau found that elderly populations have a high negative correlation with school-aged children. Sclar's (1976) study of Boston and Myers' (1978) study of the San Francisco-Oakland SMSA found similar relationships. The latter also found a high positive correlation between pre-1940 housing and elderly concentrations.[8] Since a concentration of school-aged children indicates a lack of elderly in the area, school district data delineating residential areas for these children can conceivably be used as an indicator of areas with low numbers of elderly.

Historical data analysis. Often planners rely exclusively on the most recent Census to develop a profile and understanding of the community. Because Census data is readily available back to the turn of the century, it can provide a unique historical perspective for data analysis. Because census tract data has been reported within reasonably stable boundaries since 1940, data on the age structure of a community can easily be traced over a 30-year period. Concentrations of the elderly can be identified at each Census period. Patterns and trends in the data can be explored to gain an understanding of a community's development. Extrapolating these trends into the future can help to predict service needs in particular geographic areas. Historical data analysis conducted on the text communities in this study showed that for both cities the same tracts had the highest concentrations of elderly from 1940 through the present. Figures 2 and 3 demonstrate changes in elderly population concentrations over time.

The data presented in Figures 2 and 3 suggest that the central tracts in this community may continue to have the highest concentrations of elderly in 1980. Other trends which may appear when mapping similar data include movement in a particular geographic direction (north, southwest, etc.); dispersion (distribution of elderly becoming more equal); or concentration (particular areas increase while others decrease or remain the same).

Age-cohort analysis. An age cohort is a group of people born at the same period of time. Grouping populations by cohort assumes that there are similarities in addition to age between members of the group. Members of a cohort are influenced by history; they are educated, advance their careers, and raise their families as peers in time. While an urban older person in the 1960's was likely to be a European immigrant, today a member of the same cohort would most likely be a native-born white; in the future a larger percentage will be minorities.

Figure 2
Glendale Population Density Change 1940–1950

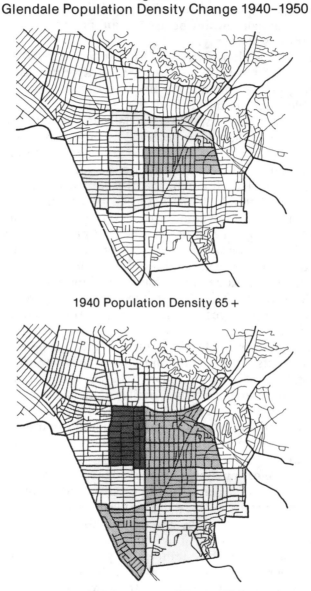

1940 Population Density 65 +

1950 Population Density 65 +

Census Tract Population 65 + (percent)

☐ 0–10%   ☐ 10–14%   ▨ 14–18%

Source: 1940 and 1950 Census of Population

Figure 3
Glendale Population Density Change 1960–1970

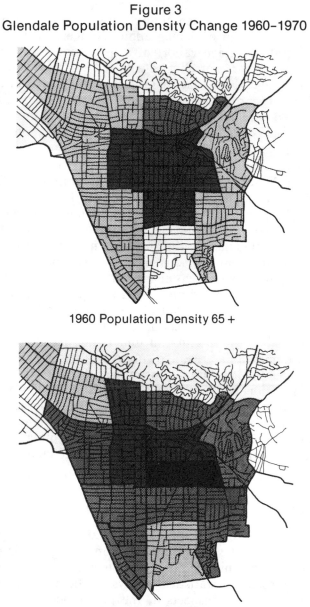

1960 Population Density 65 +

1970 Population Density 65 +

 18–22%　　　　 22–26%　　　　26 + %

Source: 1960 and 1970 Census of Population

One of the fundamental applications of age-cohort analysis is examination of demographic changes: births, deaths, and migration.[9] Each cohort of a given age, sex, and race has a survival or mortality rate based on the likelihood of persons in that group reaching the next age group. Life tables which report current survival and/or mortality rates, historical rates, and forecasts of future rates are published for the whole United States and for each state by the National Center for Health Statistics.[10]

Age-cohort data can be obtained from current and previous Censes. An example of a community's age distribution for male population from 1940 to 1970 is shown in Table 3. By following a row across the page, changes in age group size over time can be identified. By applying the survival rate to the initial population, the analyst can estimate for the next period the number of persons in the cohort expected to remain in the city if there were no migration. The difference between the actual and expected number is an estimate of net cohort migration (either into or out of the community). The line in Table 3 indicates one age cohort over time.

In addition to gaining an understanding of the population dynamics of an area, age-cohort analysis may be used for three types of population projections. The first simply ages the population in place (the survival and fertility rates are applied to the population without regard to migration). The second adds historical migration to the calculation. The third adds expected migration rates based on some other knowledge of the community (availability of developable land or changes in economic base).

Summary and Implications for Planning

A considerable amount of statistical data can be obtained from a variety of sources in every community. This chapter has presented a number of simple techniques which do not require mastery of statistical analysis. These can be used to understand various aspects of the population. The analyses presented can be categorized as either static or dynamic approaches to population analysis. The social-indicators approach, focusing on current discrete bits of information that

Table 3

Age Distribution of Male Population
of Pasadena, California, 1940 to 1970[1]

Age	1940	1950	1960	1970
0- 4	1850	3776	4699	4011
5- 9	1968	3147	4180	4178
10-14	2345	2366	3886	4142
15-19	2855	2651	3511	4322
20-24	3202	3463	3728	4844
25-29	2972	3675	3436	4108
30-34	2499	3329	3192	3379
35-39	2554	3329	3456	2282
40-44	2456	3316	3272	2967
45-49	2528	3127	3366	3028
50-54	2430	3056	3287	3114
55-59	2188	2778	3192	2810
60-64	1887	2364	2686	2529
65-69	1620	2303	2318	2212
70-74	1313	1601	1918	1540
75 +	1539	2143	2628	2727

[1]*Sources:* 1940, 1950, 1960, and 1970 Censes of Population.
Note: Line follows one age cohort over time.

explain the status of the elderly, is an example of the static approach. Age-cohort analysis, with its attention to the structural changes in the population, exemplifies the dynamic.

The dynamic approach, when used with social indicators, is important because it enables the agency to base its funding decisions on timely data rather than data from a Population Census which may be eight to ten years old. The use of subtract data, specifically *5th Count Census Block Group* data, provides a powerful method for targeting more specific areas of need. The specific needs and abilities of the analyst will determine the aspects of the analysis which are important or useful. Examples of how an agency may utilize some of the data sources introduced in this chapter follow.

SSI data. SSI information can identify changes in the size of the elderly population in poverty. Using quarterly reports of Medicare and SSI data, updating of an annual plan and determination of seasonal variation are possible. Table 2 demonstrates how to use this data to update poverty level statistics.

Sub-tract analysis. An agency might choose to conduct two or three levels of analysis. Census tract and/or zip code level data can be used in a general analysis such as identifying major geographic target areas. Sub-tract analysis can be used within these target areas to identify the specific areas and populations which have the greatest need. Focusing the analysis in such a manner can identify very specific target areas and target groups without the investment of time and resources required for sub-tract analysis of the entire metropolitan area.

Integrating housing facilities and convalescent hospitals. The location of senior housing and nursing homes may have a tremendous influence on a community's population structure. The opening and closing of such facilities may be responsible for observed population changes. Institutionalized older people are not separated in Census counts, therefore, a separate accounting is necessary to target programs for these groups. The number and distribution of institutionalized people may be important when initiating a friendly visiting project.

Secondary analyses can provide updated planning information which can be instituted in a continual process of updating projected program needs and evaluating the accuracy of previous predictions. The techniques introduced in this chapter can become the primary elements in a rudimentary planning process model.

References

Myers, D. Aging population and housing: A new perspective on planning for more balanced metropolitan growth. *Growth and Change*, January 1978, *9*(1), 8–13.

Sclar, E. D. Aging and residential location. In M. P. Lawton, R. J. Newcomer, & T. O. Byerts (Eds.), *Planning for an aging society*. Stroudsburg, Pa.: Dowden, Hutchinson & Ross, 1976.

U. S. Bureau of the Census. *1940 Census Tract Reports*. (PHC (1)) LA–LB SMSA.

U. S. Bureau of the Census. *1950 Census Tract Reports.* (PHC (1)) LA-LB SMSA.

U. S. Bureau of the Census. *1960 Census Tract Reports.* (PHC (1)) LA-LB SMSA.

U. S. Bureau of the Census. *1970 Census Tract Reports.* (PHC (1)) LA-LB SMSA.

U. S. Government Accounting Office. *The well-being of older people in Cleveland, Ohio.* Washington, D.C.: U.S. Government Printing Office, 1977.

United Way. *Planning for the aging.* Los Angeles County United Way Region III. Los Angeles: United Way, 1973.

[1]Examples of reports generated from census data are the United Way Planning documents. *Planning for the Aging: Los Angeles County United Way. Regions I and II.* These documents include Glendale and Pasadena, our test communities. They were financed by the California Department on Aging prior to the establishment of the Area Agency network. The census data used in these reports included age, poverty, and ethnicity.

[2]Aggregation is the process of combining information into fewer categories; disaggregation involves dividing data into smaller, more distinct categories.

[3]It is recommended that persons wishing to use the Census consult additional sources. The following Census publications are available at most public libraries:

U.S. Department of Commerce, *Reference Manual on Population and Housing Statistics from the Census Bureau.*

Designed to provide a comprehensive introduction to demographic data, it is available from the Census Bureau. This is the best starting place for the novice. (Available from Subscriber Services Section, Bureau of the Census, Washington, D.C. 20233).

U.S. Department of Commerce, *1970 Census Users' Guide* (Parts I and II). October 1970.

Part I explains how the Census is collected and processed, indicates what is generally available from each Census source, and includes sample tables from the major printed reports. A dictionary of Census concepts and technical terms is included.

Part II describes the *Census Summary Tapes*, explains how to access Census data from computer tapes, and lists the specific tables which are stored in the first four counts. Useful Census data available from summary tapes are listed in the appendix.

U.S. Department of Commerce, *Census User's Workshop Manual.*

This is a detailed volume prepared for workshops conducted by the Census Bureau. It shows examples of the data from all counts of the Census, explains the various levels of aggregation, describes the data available at each level, and provides examples of potential uses of Census data.

⁴One must exercise caution in the use of SSI data. Some cross-tabulations aggregate the blind and disabled under 65 with the aged. Separate counts by age are normally available, however.

⁵U.S. Department of Commerce, *Current Population Reports*, Series P-28, "Special Censes," published periodically.

Six-month summaries of the special censes conducted by the Census Bureau are published twice each year. Each special census is printed as part of the series upon its completion and is available from the Census Bureau for a nominal charge.

⁶The Special Census conducted in Pasadena included 10 socioeconomic questions not asked in Glendale. Five-year age cohorts at the block group and census tract levels are available from both communities and for any other city which participated with the California Department of Finance.

⁷The Census variable is unrelated individuals. Information on the sex and economic status of unrelated individuals over 65 is available from the Census. Use of this information allows one to compare the relative status of the elderly living alone with those in families and other household types.

⁸The R^2 for the relationship between pre-1940 housing and the elderly in Oakland was .81. It is important to remember that a high positive correlation in one community does not necessarily mean the same relationship will be true in other communities.

⁹Pittenger, D. B. *Projecting state and local populations*. Cambridge, Mass.: Ballinger, 1976. Chapter 5 through 9 detail the procedures and considerations involved in using age cohort data to project the age and sex compositions of future populations.

¹⁰Available from the U.S. Government Printing Office and most major libraries.

3

HISTORICAL AND CONTEXTUAL DATA ANALYSIS TECHNIQUES

Rex Painter
and Carol Ohlrogge

*Rex Painter is the Planner for the Council on
Aging of Santa Clara County, Incorporated,
San Jose, California.*

*Carol Ohlrogge is Project Director for the East
Los Angeles Historic Preservation Project of
TELACU, Los Angeles, California.*

Introduction

History is the recording of human behavior through time. Historical accounts provide an expression of social direction as well as portray the foundations of today's attitudes, political sentiments, and economic structure. This chapter will demonstrate the ways historical information can provide a context for current planning activity, a context especially pertinent when considering service programs for the elderly, who have experienced historical change,and whose attitudes have been shaped by these changes. To design service programs for elderly populations, planners must be familiar with the development of a community and its attitudes.

Those responsible for service delivery planning traditionally rely on census information to specify service programs. Census information, however, cannot supply the contextual details of a community's development and unique attitudes. Use of historical data in planning analysis provides an inexpensive and easy-to-access source rich in contextual information.

Improving the State of the Art

Historical data can best be used to establish a detailed community profile. A profile can improve the planning function by providing a clear sense or "feel" for a community's development. When used in conjunction with traditional planning techniques, this profile can provide a much more comprehensive view of a planning service area.

A community profile based on various readily available historical materials establishes a means of determining the character or personality of a particular community. A community is defined in part by its physical area, but is also distinguished by a unique character which stems from a variety of other factors, such as the people who inhabit the community or its economic conditions. Examining the history of the community allows the planner to better understand the subtleties of continuing change. The structure of the community, including its people and their attitudes, provides the context for this development.

In conducting a historical analysis, it is important to identify community changes that have strongly influenced community growth. These changes can be displayed by using several techniques that provide a visual image of the community's changing character. Together, these techniques form the historical and contextual profile which will allow the planner to better understand and visualize the forces within a community.

Data Search

Initially, one must identify data sources which provide historical information about the community's social and physical development. An excellent source for this information would be the spokesperson for the historical society or the reference librarian for the local city library. In preparing for an extensive analysis, the planner should develop a list of research questions. These should focus on the social forces which prompted the settlement of the area, the social and economic status of the settlers, the formation of local government, and the civic and service clubs which were influential in city development.

Table 1 details a list of potential data sources rated by usefulness. The value or usefulness of each source will depend on the cost of accessing the data as well as to its ultimate contribution toward a comprehensive analysis, and may vary depending on the community being studied.

Those resources determined to be highly useful provide data that is easily accessed, relevant, and of good quality. For example, local chronologies provide a quick overview of events perceived by the community as important and influential in its development. Those sources designated as marginally useful provide less data and are not universally available or accessible; some also require the researcher to deal with local bureaucracies, sorting through a number of unrelated documents.

Table 1

Usefulness Potential of Data Resources

Data Source	Usefulness	Some Expected Information
Census of Population	High	Population, Number of Families, Personal Income, Ethnic Breakdown, Age Breakdown
City Planning Documents	High	Historical Preservation Element, Past Planning Concerns, Chronology, Annexation Map, Economic Base Information
Local Historical Chronologies	High	Biographies of Long-time Residents, Historical Interests of the Community
City and County Data Book	High	Ethnic Breakdown, Personal Income, Community Economic Base Information
Local Histories	High	Local History and Community Background
Oral Historical Accounts	High	Subjective View of the Community, Political and Ethnic Characteristics, Supplemental Information
County Registrar of Voters	High	Total Number of Registered Voters, Number of Democrats, Republicans and Others

City Clerk's Office	Marginal	List of Municipal Acquisitions by Year and Description
Chamber of Commerce	Marginal	Some Economic Growth Data, Promotional Chronology, Possible Biographical Information About Local Notables
Community Development Reports	Marginal	Possible Data on Annexations, Economic Base or Ethnicity
Biographies of Local Notables	Marginal	Biographical Information on Influential Residents
Local and Regional Newspapers	Marginal	Community Interest and Response to Issues and Changes

Analytical Methods

The most appropriate analytical methods for a historical analysis are those that pinpoint significant past developments and trace the effects of those developments. A constructed historical perspective will clarify special characteristics of proposed programs inappropriate or unacceptable to the community.

Three mechanisms can be used to gain insight into the subtleties of a community's character: the historical time line, maturity patterns, and oral histories. The following briefly defines each method.

Historical time line. Local written histories can be plotted or mapped using events which indicate major community changes. Such events can be classified as producing social or physical impacts. Items of particular interest could include major political decisions, community-wide events, large-scale physical or economic changes, or racial integration controversies.

Maturity patterns. Maturity patterns will provide supplemental information concerning an area's development and growth, and may include spatial, political, and economic changes in the community. The mapping of municipal property acquisition is one example. Similarly, the graphing of economic changes, political party affiliations, and ethnic composition make it possible to examine changes in the socio-political environment.

Oral histories. Oral histories are the systematic recording of remembered and experienced events from interviews with residents. They usually provide unpublished accounts of community development and are useful for augmenting written histories and maturity patterns. The success of this technique depends on the quality of community "knowledgeables" selected to review the community history. Such individuals should be long-time residents with involvement in civic or governmental affairs.

Figure 1 lists the data sources identified in Table 1, suggesting their relative applicability to the analytical methods described above.

Figure 1
Applicability of Data Resources to Analysis Techniques

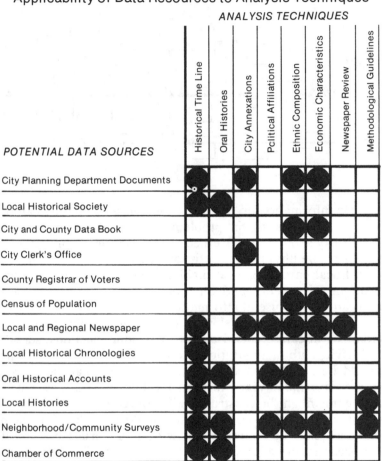

Historical Time Line

The primary information sources for a time line are readily accessible local written histories. Generally these documents are found in special collections or reference sections of the local community library. Historical publications provide a comprehensive knowledge base from which a community profile can be constructed. Publications that provide

Figure 2
Historical Time Line

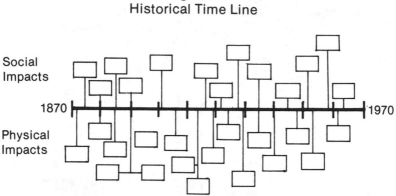

Social
Impacts

1870 ———————————————————— 1970

Physical
Impacts

reliable information on community evolution generally can be located by discussing the problem with the librarian. Ideally, the history should be concerned with social development as it relates to the physical and attitudinal changes of the community. Local chronologies available in municipal publications, planning documents, and Chamber of Commerce pamphlets also can provide useful information.

The first step in developing a time line is collecting a record of significant events. Items such as bond elections, service and civic club inaugurations, and community-wide events should be noted on 3 x 5 cards. These cards can be placed on the time line in yearly increments. Figure 2 illustrates how a time line might be constructed. To overcome the problem of excessive data, the local librarian should be enlisted to help the researcher determine which written materials best meet the needs of the analysis. Generally the guidelines are comprehensiveness, community focus, and level of developmental detail. Information should be reviewed carefully to insure focus on changes and events which were most influential in the community's development.

Maturity Patterns

Maturity patterns provide the planner with an impression of how the community has changed historically. Information

Figure 3
Glendale Annexation Patterns

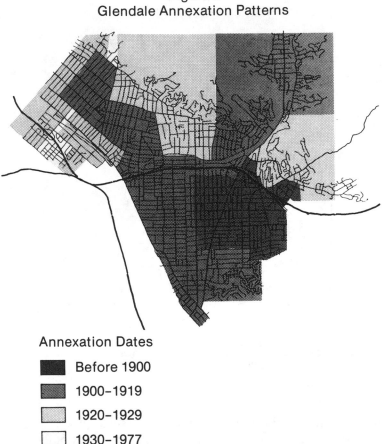

Annexation Dates

⬛	Before 1900
▨	1900–1919
▫	1920–1929
⬜	1930–1977

sources will vary depending on the type and sophistication of descriptive data desired. Data on physical growth, political party affiliation, ethnic composition, and economic characteristics are typical measures that are readily available.

Annexations. The physical growth of a city can be mapped by locating annexation and municipal property acquisitions as illustrated in Figure 3. City planning and community development departments maintain annexation maps showing parcels divided by year of acquisition. The mapping

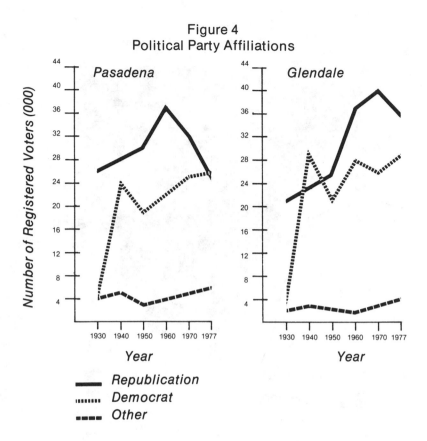

Figure 4
Political Party Affiliations

Pasadena

Glendale

Number of Registered Voters (000)

Year

Year

━━━ *Republication*
▪▪▪▪▪ *Democrat*
▬ ▬ ▬ *Other*

of annexations will show the scale of physical growth and the direction of that growth. Such mapping identifies older areas of the city that could include dilapidated housing and higher concentrations of elderly populations.

Political party affiliation. Political party affiliation data, available from the County Registrar of Voters, can provide a measure of political change over time. Although inadequate for in-depth political analysis of a community, this information permits a general characterization of the community which could indicate potential problems in community acceptance of publicly sponsored programs. By calculating the total number of registered voters for each party in 10-year increments, trends in the community are easily visualized, as demonstrated in Figure 4.

Economic characteristics. Economic data available from the *Census of Population* will provide a gross indication of changes in community and personal income levels and sources. To show shifts in family income, the total number of families should be obtained from the *Census of Population* along with the number of families below poverty level and the number above middle income for each census year. Data should be mathematically adjusted to account for inflationary effects on the dollar. The exact dollar amounts assigned for poverty level and upper income are not critical as long as the system of classification remains consistent. The total number of families and the number in the lower, middle, and upper income ranges can then be displayed, as illustrated in Figure 5.

Maturity Pattern Analysis

After maturity data is compiled and displayed, patterns of community character will emerge. Shifts in one category may be reflected by changes in another. Annexations, for example, may account for shifts in ethnic, political, and economic characteristics. Consider the implications for change in census data if a community were to annex an unincorporated area consisting of a large minority population or an industrial park area. Maturity patterns will not only provide a visual means for conceptualizing the community character and personality, but also will raise questions for inclusion in oral interviews.

The information obtained as outlined above will indicate general community trends and is easily accessible. The data may reach as far back in time as desired; however, the year 1930 appears to be an optimal starting point for several reasons. First, census data-gathering techniques became more sophisticated and information collected for these years will be compatible with recent censuses. Second, the Depression can be used as a base point for the oral histories. Thus, using 1930 can provide consistency and continuity for the analytical techniques.

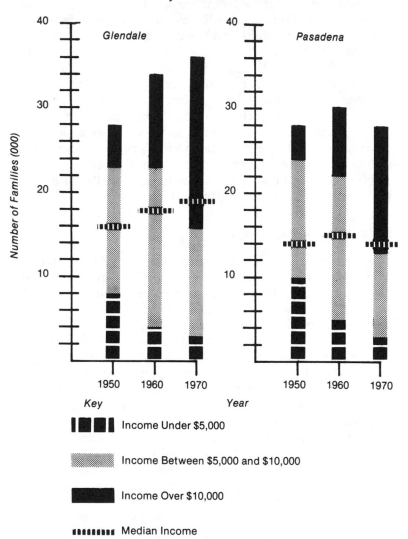

Figure 5
Family Income Levels

Key   Year

▮▮▮▮ Income Under $5,000

Income Between $5,000 and $10,000

▬ Income Over $10,000

▬▬▬ Median Income

Oral Histories

Oral histories are an important supplement to written histories and maturity patterns. Knowledgeable long-time residents are often active participants in local civic affairs. Local librarians may be able to provide biographical information on residents, thereby lending a dimension of familiarity to the interview.

Interview questions should be tailored for the particular respondent and his/her area of interest. The objective of oral interviews is to ascertain in-depth responses to changes in community attitudes and composition. One should be aware that published documents, particularly those from promotional sources, may provide information only about those events that were considered positive or a credit to the community. Events or influences which are perceived to be negative may not be given equal coverage. Oral histories can provide information about these hidden events, and also document more completely the day-to-day aspects of living in the community.

In addition to the overall community character, these interviews provide details on specific points or issues in its history. The impact of major events such as freeway completions, economic changes, and racial integration can be determined. Specific interview techniques are outlined by Baum (1974). Figure 6 provides a sample instrument that can be used to direct the interview process. The interview should be less concerned with actual dates than with eliciting recordable experiences from residents. The process is designed to stimulate conversation and recall, using the interviewees' own pace of remembering the past. Some caution must be exercised as to interview confidentiality and the legal ramifications of using information gained from oral histories.

The information obtained from oral interviews can be used to answer questions raised by the written histories and maturity patterns. These interview data will have a subjective and contextual aspect which will complement the more objective profile. These interviews should confirm or deny speculations derived from the written materials.

Figure 6
Oral History Sample Instrument

1. Name?
2. Age?
3. How long have you lived in_____?
4. What prompted you to move to the area?
   Or, what prompted you to remain in the area?
5. What was your main occupaton?
6. How would you characterize your stay in_____?
7. What institutional changes would you say have influenced the city?
8. How would you describe the racial climate in your community?
9. What group of individual residents has been most influential in the city's development?
10. How has the community changed since 1930? Since World War II?
11. Do you feel your community is unique to other communities in the area?
12.[1] How have the following events influenced the community overall?

[1] This question should relate to specific events which have been identified from the community's written history.

Technique Utility

When all three analytical techniques are combined in a systematic fashion, the planner will gain a detailed documented profile of community changes. These data analyses can be used independently of one another or in combination. However, the application of a single technique may produce an incomplete profile of the community. For example, the use of oral histories alone may establish a personalized, highly subjective account of perceived change and development. In some instances, time constraints may preclude the use of all three techniques; therefore, the value of each is discussed separately.

The *historical time line* is the most comprehensive technique. Data used for this analysis are readily available. One drawback to this approach is the amount of time required for data access and display. Written histories tend to focus on major trends; thus a careful search for subtle indicators of community change is necessary.

Maturity patterns do not integrate historical information. However, they do isolate relevant data useful for familiarizing the researcher with sociopolitical changes in a community. The major limitation of this approach is the ingenuity and interest of the researcher. Data displayed for various descriptive variables can be tailored to a particular community problem. For example, an area with a primary agricultural base may suggest rural to urban population shifts.

The *oral history technique* provides the researcher with a personalized interpretation of an area's history. Data gathered through an interview process draws on the experiences of community residents. This approach works best as an adjunct to the first two techniques. It will answer elusive questions raised by the other approaches, fill information gaps, and clarify the impact of specific events. It does, however, require that the interviewer develop a specific set of questions and be able to direct the interview process. Preparation of historical data-based questions and knowledge of interviewing techniques are essential.

Each technique has advantages and disadvantages. A systematic integration of the information using all three techniques will produce a very adequate profile of the community. The integration procedure used will depend on the specific objectives of the researcher, but should be directed toward combining data that indicate social and attitudinal changes in the community.

Summary

Much historical data and information can be obtained from a variety of community sources. The research reported here describes three simple techniques which can be used to create a community historical profile. These techniques do not require special analytical skills in order to provide a useful document for service planners.

In constructing a historical data profile, it is not the physical product itself that provides insights into the community character, but rather the process of data acquisition. As in all of the historical analysis techniques, knowledge is derived from the process of synthesizing various sources of data into a coherent pattern.

These community characterizations cannot be developed from traditional data sources and data-gathering techniques. Traditional methods utilizing secondary census data are largely incapable of describing the subtle aspects of community development and character. Because of the level of expertise or sophistication and the minimal time required, the historical and contextual profile is a feasible means to provide planners with an often overlooked perspective of the community. Where it is not possible to follow every step in this methodology due to realistic constraints, the three analytical techniques may be used independently.

Implications

After completing this type of historical and contextual investigation, the crucial question is, "What has been gained? What information has been learned and how can it be used?" Perhaps the best way to answer this is to point out what has *not* been gained. Historical analysis of this type will not provide a complete analysis of local history; it will not provide answers to or make decisions about specific contemporary problems. The historical and contextual profile *will* provide an intuitive and subtle "feel" for the community environment. This "feel" will provide the practitioner with a historical perspective that can be used in the planning and decisionmaking process.

The purpose of the analysis is to broaden the knowledge base of the planning and research practitioner by using community historical data. This type of data is readily available, easily utilized, and highly applicable for community analysis. The analytical approach reviewed has relevance for those practitioners concerned with the development of historical preservation programs, the development of neighborhoods, the salience of community organizations, resolution of intra-community conflicts, community revitalization needs, and integration of the community service network. The value of this type of analysis is the development of a background profile of the community, use of which is limited only by the imagination, insight, ability, and interest of the practitioner.

A basic understanding of the community, its structure, and its character is an important part of the planning process. By developing and using this type of knowledge, the planner or program designer can better understand the community context in which the delivery of services must take place. Furthermore, this context can suggest indicators of service needs as well as levels and types of intervention that may be feasible. This may facilitate not only community acceptance, but ultimately the success of a particular proposal by fitting the design of the services to the character of the elderly community.

References

Baum, W. K. *Oral history for the local historical society.* Nashville, Tenn.: American Association for State and Local History, 1974.

4

PHYSICAL FORM AND LAND-USE ANALYSIS TECHNIQUES

four

Jill Glenn,
Susan Alley,
and Keith Shirasawa

Jill Glenn is completing dual graduate degrees in Gerontology and Urban and Regional Planning at the University of Southern California, Los Angeles, California.

Susan Alley holds a student professional position with the Department of Community Development, County of Los Angeles, Los Angeles, California.

Keith Shirasawa is a Planner with Gerontological Planning Associates, Santa Monica, California.

Introduction

The topographical and land-use characteristics of an urban area have a direct effect on the ability of older people to support themselves independently. Older people, more than any other age group, are left at the mercy of the physical environment: steep hills, uncommonly long distances to supportive goods and services, and busy traffic. These are only a few of the factors that influence the older person's ability to maintain independence. At the same time, pronounced limitations on mobility are stimulated by an increased level of chronic and debilitating ailments. For a variety of reasons, older persons experience the environment more directly than do others and are, as a consequence, more vulnerable.

Despite the importance of these conditions, service planners are generally unfamiliar with the techniques and information sources available that detail these environmental qualities. The purpose of this chapter is to familiarize the planner with the techniques available to analyze the physical environment in order to specify more appropriate program interventions. Familiarity with the concepts and methods outlined in this chapter will provide another means of supplementing conventional secondary data analyses.

Improving the State of the Art

There is no tradition of land-use and/or topographical analysis for planning and evaluating services for older people. Many service planners have a social welfare background and are not well-acquainted with the types of techniques and information sources readily available which can facilitate their familiarity with a target area.

Urban planners regularly rely upon a number of methods and information sources to determine land-use patterns, and these information sources are readily available and understandable by individuals with little experience in land-use planning.

Some of the techniques and information sources available include the following: zoning and land-use maps, aerial photographs, windshield surveys, and walking tours. All of these can be useful to the service planner. These information sources require little or no alteration and are readily available from other agencies. The next section will specifically demonstrate and explain how these city planning techniques can be transferred for use in planning supportive services for older urban neighborhood dwellers. Special care has been taken to present methods that are time and labor efficient.

Beginning with zoning maps which offer the least amount of detail and ending with a land-use classification method which is based on the exact type of activity, this section will demonstrate how each method builds upon and supplements those which preceeded it.

Zoning Maps

Zoning, a means by which city planners control urban growth and development, specifies the types of activities that may or may not occur within a certain area. Through zoning, situations such as an elementary school being placed next door to a busy shopping center are avoided.

In addition to separating such mutually antagonistic land uses from one another, development density and growth may be controlled through zoning. In most cities throughout the United States every land parcel has a zoning designation. City planning departments are charged with the responsibility of updating existing documentation.

Issues in zoning. Zoning maps are not totally reliable as an accurate representation of an urban area because (1) these maps indicate maximum *allowable* (not *actual*) use; (2) zoning measures may be overridden by means of variances which are special exemptions to the legal use. For these reasons, zoning maps when considered alone are not a wholly reliable source of land-use distribution. Zoning maps such as the Glendale example in Figure 1 are available from either city planning or zoning departments in most cities.

Figure 1
Glendale Target Area Zoning Designations

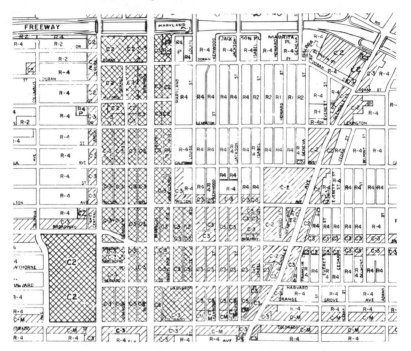

ZONE	LEGEND		
R1R	RESTRICTED ONE-FAMILY	C1	RESTRICTED COMMERCIAL
R1	ONE-FAMILY	C2	LIMITED COMMERCIAL
R2	THREE-FAMILY	C3	COMMERCIAL
RE	LIMITED MULTIPLE DWELLING	CM	COMMERCIAL-MANUFACTURING
R3R	RESTRICTED LIMITED MULTIPLE	CA	COMMERCIAL-AGRICULTURAL
	DWELLING	MIA	SPECIAL RESTRICTED INDUSTRIAL
R4	MULTIPLE DWELLING	M1	RESTRICTED INDUSTRIAL
R4L	RESTRICTED MULTIPLE DWELLING	M2	INDUSTRIAL
R5	HIGH DENSITY MULTIPLE DWELLING	M3	HEAVY INDUSTRIAL
P	PARKING (OVERLAY ZONE)	H	HORSE (OVERLAY ZONE)
PRC	PLANNED RESIDENTIAL CLUSTER	CEM	CEMETERY (OVERLAY ZONE)
PRD	PLANNED RESIDENTIAL DEVELOP-	SR	SPECIAL RECREATION
	MENT (OVERLAY ZONE)		
PUD	PLANNED UNIT DEVELOPMENT		
	(OVERLAY ZONE)		

FIRE ZONE NO. 1

FIRE ZONE NO. 2

FIRE ZONE NO. 3

Source: Planning Division,
City of Glendale

Figure 2
Land Use Classifications

			Prismacolor
RESIDENTIAL			
Single-family	SF	☐	915 Lemon Yellow
2-family	2F	☐	939 Flesh (or 942)
3- and 4-family	34F	☐	917 Yellow Orange
Boarding and rooming houses	BH	☐	943 Burnt Ochre
Multiple dwelling (over 4-family)	APT	☐	946 Dark Brown
Tourists and trailer courts	T	☐	930 Magenta
Hotel	H	☐	931 Purple
BUSINESS & COMMERCIAL			
Local (neighborhood) business	LB	☐	929 Pink
Offices and banks	OB	☐	921 Vermilion Red
General business	GB	☐	923 Scarlet Lake
Intensive business, theatres, recreation	IB	☐	925 Crimson Lake
INDUSTRIAL			
Light industry	LM	☐	964 Light Gray
Railroads and public utilities	PM	☐	962 Dark Gray
Heavy industry	HM	☐	935 Black

			Prismacolor
PUBLIC			
Parks	P	☐	910 True Green
Public schools	P	☐	909 Grass Green
Public buildings	P	☐	903 Dark Green
QUASI-PUBLIC			
Quasi-public open uses	QP	☐	903 True Blue (or 904)
Churches	QP	☐	902 Ultramarine
Quasi-public buildings & institutions	QP	☐	901 Indigo Blue
Cemeteries	QP	☐	905 Aquamarine
AGRICULTURAL			
Crop land	AC	☐	912 Apple Green
Livestock land	AL	☐	911 Olive Green
MINING			
	E	☐	No color
VACANT LAND			
	V	☐	No color

SOURCE: *Mapping for Planning Publication No. 101 Public Administration Service, Chicago, Ill.*

Note: Colors refer to prismacolor pencil designations.

Land-use Maps

While zoning maps display allowable legal maximums and types of uses, land-use maps portray actual uses in an urban area. Figure 2 lists the typical categorizations of land-use maps. Land-use maps are not part of any enabling legislation, as are zoning maps. Where zoning maps are prescriptive and backed by legal sanctions, land-use maps are merely descriptive, with no legal clout.

Land-use issues. Accurate, current land-use maps are extremely rare in many planning departments. It requires a great deal of time to collect land-use data on a lot-by-lot basis, and once complete, it takes almost as much time to maintain and update these maps. Detailed land-use maps are generally collected only on a project-by-project basis. Land-use maps, when available, can be secured from city planning departments.

The actual utility of these two data sources, that is, zoning maps and land-use maps, lies in comparing the two. This comparison will reveal areas within a neighborhood that are "underbuilt." This condition exists, for example, where a single family residence (SFR) is located in an area zoned for large apartments. The SFR is likely to be acquired, demolished, and replaced with an apartment. This becomes a concern of the Area Agency planner when large concentrations of older people reside in these underbuilt areas. Should a planner determine from secondary census data that older people are residing in large numbers in an unstable area, he can begin to take measures to lessen the impact of any future relocation that may occur as the area changes.

General Plan Maps

Another means of predicting development growth is based on consulting general plan maps. Intended as guides for long term development, these documents can reveal where future development and growth is expected.

Characteristics of general plans. Typically, these documents are intended to be in effect for up to 30 years. To maintain relevance for such a period of time, general plans are necessarily written in broad, non-specific terms. These general plans are not intended to serve as guides for specific development on a block-by-block basis. Where a zoning map would describe an area in terms of specific allowable uses such as shown in Figure 1, a general plan map would project land uses for the same area in broader, less specific terms, such as the 1990 Glendale land-use plan illustrated in Figure 3.

General plan maps do not provide an accurate representation of existing land uses or zoning; however, they do provide specific guidelines that will channel future land development. These materials are also available for public review and distribution at local city planning agency offices.

Soliciting data from planning agencies. If approached with the appropriate questions, planning office personnel can provide a wealth of information. Asking the right questions may ease the task of an Area Agency planner having to deal with an unfamiliar area. Specific areas of inquiry could include major residential locations of elderly, high elderly population concentrations, future areas of elderly population concentration, familiar and frequently utilized goods and services, and topographically varied districts and planning areas that are currently undergoing population or housing changes (such as condominium conversion) which might affect the elderly.

Aerial Photography Analysis

Aerial photographs are among the most useful devices a planner can use to develop a comprehensive image of a target area (Branch, 1971; Wronski & Davies, 1972). Although the photo does not classify areas as does a zoning map, one can discern open space, undeveloped areas, street widths, and other visual elements not shown on other representations. The planner can develop a general "feel" for the layout of a target area while maintaining a sense of the total region. The physical structures and street grid viewed on an aerial may indicate special areas that warrant more detailed study.

Aerial photographs represent the most efficient means of both verifying and updating land-use and zoning maps. An aerial photograph such as the Glendale map illustrated in

Figure 3
Glendale 1990 General Land Use Plan

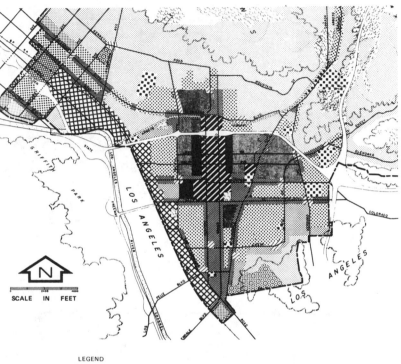

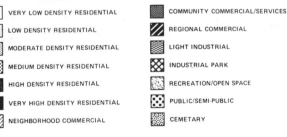

LEGEND

☐ VERY LOW DENSITY RESIDENTIAL		▨ COMMUNITY COMMERCIAL/SERVICES	
▨ LOW DENSITY RESIDENTIAL		▨ REGIONAL COMMERCIAL	
▨ MODERATE DENSITY RESIDENTIAL		▨ LIGHT INDUSTRIAL	
▨ MEDIUM DENSITY RESIDENTIAL		▨ INDUSTRIAL PARK	
▮ HIGH DENSITY RESIDENTIAL		▨ RECREATION/OPEN SPACE	
▮ VERY HIGH DENSITY RESIDENTIAL		▨ PUBLIC/SEMI-PUBLIC	
▨ NEIGHBORHOOD COMMERCIAL		▨ CEMETARY	

Source: Planning Division, City of Glendale
Land Use Element, 1976

Figure 4
Glendale Target Area Aerial Photograph

Source: Aerial photograph by Metrex Management Corporation, Los Angeles.

Figure 4 can be compared to zoning or land-use maps. Visual comparison can quickly identify underbuilt areas that exist.

Aerial photographs, while providing the physical layout of the city, can also give the service planner a great deal of socioeconomic, institutional, and qualitative information on the environment applicable to the elderly. Data from aerial photos include the following:

1. Roof size (indicating building size)
2. Open space (including parking)
3. Street width, cross walks (representing potential barriers to older pedestrians)
4. Tire markings on streets (including nearby streets)
5. Shadow pattern (indicating building height)

Small dwelling units in close proximity might indicate low value residential land. Population densities can also be estimated from the type of housing found in an area. Commercial strip development can be analyzed with regard to residential areas. Comparative analysis of aerial photos taken of the same neighborhood at different time intervals can provide an indication of land development or vegetational change. State transportation or land reclamation departments often have aerial photographs. This information may be applicable for future development, particularly in low-income or deteriorating portions of a community.

Planners interested in providing services to the elderly will benefit most from an aerial photograph. The distances between various land forms in the environment can be measured against the use of the environment by the elderly. Wide streets which act as pedestrian barriers can be identified. Parking lots that may be conducive to street crime can be identified. Service planners can use aerials to identify potential problem areas or to identify routes for the targeting of small scale transportation systems. Existing service centers for the elderly can be noted and analyzed for potential coordination with other service centers.

Aerial photographs represent a special resource to Area Agency planners, who almost always work in understaffed organizations, because they quickly reveal a great deal of contextual information.

Windshield Surveys

After a target area has been identified on an aerial map, a windshield survey can be utilized to compile detailed information about a specific environment. This simple method entails a drive or walk through the target neighborhood to determine the layout and interrelationships of:

1. Commercial strips
2. Residential districts
3. Green spaces or parks
4. Other open spaces
5. Industrial areas
6. Areas that generate specialized functions (such as hospitals and churches)
7. Blighted and deteriorating areas
8. Conflicts between pedestrians and vehicles

Windshield surveys are the most time-consuming, yet accurate, technique for analyzing land uses. A windshield survey can be used to check information from an aerial or to develop reliable indicators of conditions not immediately apparent from aerial photographs.

Documentation of a windshield survey can take many forms. Various elements can be noted verbally, sketched, or photographed. Photographic analysis is preferred to other recording methods for several reasons. Photography provides economical and comprehensive access to visually observable aspects of the environment. Human behavior and environmental forms can be recorded and analyzed with photography without loss due to observer error, limitations of observer skill, or speed of recording.

Although photography is the preferred method of documentation, a windshield survey is commonly recorded with simple notes written while the survey progresses. A specific application of this technique follows in the next section.

Classifying Land-use for Planning for the Elderly

This section provides a means of measuring and recording the supportiveness of existing land-use patterns within target areas. Conventional land-use categories are too broad to be useful to the service planner wishing to measure the responsiveness of existing land-use patterns to the needs of older community residents. Standard land-use classifications typically consist of designations that separate parcels into general categories. Rarely are distinctions made within each category. No distinction is made between land uses that are more or less likely to be utilized by older people. However, the isolation and identification of land uses supportive of seniors is essential in the planning, targeting, and evaluation of transportation alternatives.

Methodology. The most efficient method of measuring the supportiveness of existing land-use patterns is to conduct a windshield survey of the target area and identify those uses that would most likely support activities of older people. Depending on the size of the area examined, a walking tour may be used to supplement the windshield survey.

Categories can be developed to classify the existing land-use patterns so that supportive goods and services can be distinguished from those that are nonsupportive and hostile. The following categories typify this classification system:

1. *Elderly-specific supportive.* These uses include goods and services such as senior centers, elderly housing sites, nutrition and recreational sites, and any other resource designed for and utilized by an elderly client group.

2. *Non-elderly specific supportive.* These would be services such as supermarkets, pharmacies, small groceries, and banks. While not intended exclusively for older people, these goods and services are nonetheless essential to support their basic needs. This is almost always the largest category.

3. *Neutral land uses.* This category includes those uses that are of little use or interest to most older people. Examples would be record stores, ethnic and health food restaurants, stereo retailers, and other uses intended for a younger cohort.

4. *Antagonistic land uses.* This category includes any land uses which generate either real or perceived activity that acts against the interests of most older people. The most obvious examples would be those land uses that encourage criminal activity such as vacant buildings, high schools, and "dive"-like bars.

Before conducting a windshield survey, the service planner should obtain both a land-use and zoning map from the local city planning department, if available. This will allow the planner to determine the relationship between residential and commercial districts. Combining this information

Figure 5
Elderly Relevant Land Use Categories

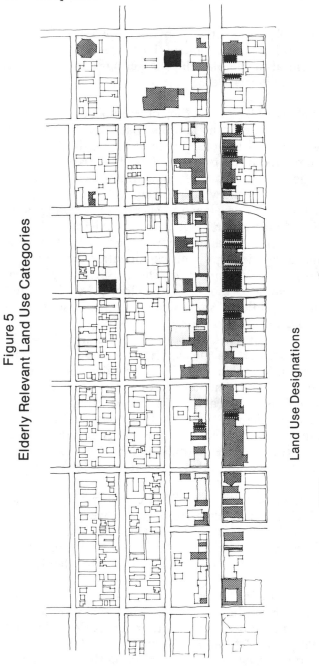

Land Use Designations

Elderly Specific-Supportive

Nonelderly Specific-Supportive

Neutral

Antagonistic

Figure 6
Commercial Residential Land Use Relationships

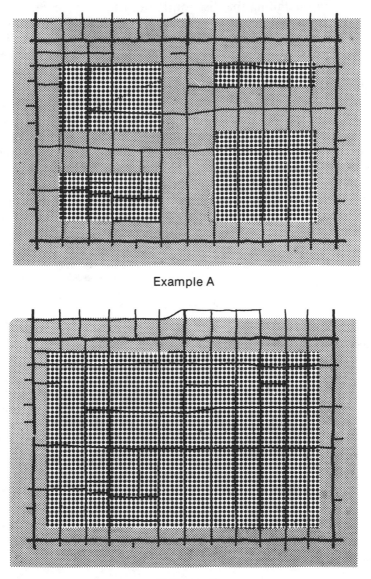

Example A

Example B

Land Use Designations

 Supportive Commercial   Elderly Residential

with a map detailing the distribution of the 60 or 65+ population, the planner will develop a sense of where the older population is located in relationship to major commercial districts. The windshield survey will then allow the identification of commercial land uses that most likely would be utilized by older residents. Figure 6 illustrates two typical commercial-residential land-use relationships.

Example A is an ubiquitous commercial layout, while Example B is a perimeter commercial district configuration. Often the perimeter pattern seen in Example B will reinforce the area within it and define it as a separate and distinct neighborhood. The "strip" pattern shown in Example A often serves to divide existing neighborhoods. This type of information allows a planner to compare neighborhood configuration with existing line haul transportation resources to determine what measures, if any, would be appropriate to facilitate the linkage between the older person's home and services.

Lynchian Landform Categories

Lynch (1960) has developed concepts and methods for classyfing and describing the urban environment that transcend the methods described in this chapter. Where land use and zoning maps are based on actual and intended uses respectively, Lynch's methods are based on the "imageability" of the environment in addition to use patterns. This method of classifying environments relies heavily on the identification of districts, landmarks, nodes, paths, and edges contained within the larger urban environment. Service planners would do well to familiarize themselves with Lynch's observational and epistomological methods, because they can be very helpful in abstracting critical features of the urban environment for further analysis and understanding.[1]

Implications

This land-use analysis is meant to be used as a supplement to conventional analytical planning techniques such as a secondary data analysis. Conventional target-area profiling techniques ignore the physical attributes of an urban environment which significantly affect the effective and efficient delivery of social services to the elderly. Service planners must realize that older people are vulnerable to and affected by the physical environment. Because older people spend more time as pedestrians, their increased exposure to the environment combined with age-related declines in stamina underscore the effect the physical environment can have on the older person.

This chapter acquaints service planners with techniques for observing and recording the environment within which services are to be delivered. In addition to sensitizing service planners to the built environment, this chapter also introduces other municipal and state-level departments which may have information about qualities of the urban physical environment.

References

Branch, M. C. *City planning and aerial information.* Cambridge, Mass.: Harvard University Press, 1971.

City of Glendale. *Preliminary draft land use element.* Glendale, Calif.: Glendale Planning Division, 1976.

Lynch, K. *The image of the city.* Cambridge, Mass.: Massachusetts Institute of Technology, 1960.

Wronski, W., & Davies, K. *Photo interpretation for planners* (Kodak Publication No. M–81). Rochester, N.Y.: Eastman Kodak Co., 1972.

---

[1]For further detail consult *The Image of the City* by Kevin Lynch. In this work Lynch develops a framework within which the classification and description of a selected area can occur. Although *The Image of the City* is not focused on the special needs of older people, it is a classic work that describes in detail a well-recognized land form classification system.

5

SERVICE INVENTORY ANALYSIS TECHNIQUES

five

Elaine Murakami,
Katherine Pellman,
and Jill Sterrett

Elaine Murakami is the recipient of a Minority Aging Fellowship, University Center on Aging, San Diego State University, and is a Research Assistant, Andrus Gerontology Center, University of Southern California.

Katherine Pellman is completing dual masters' degrees in Gerontology and Urban and Regional Planning and is a Research Assistant, Andrus Gerontology Center, University of Southern California.

Jill Sterrett is a planner with Donald A. Cotton Associates, private consultants in Urban and Environmental Planning, Pasadena, California.

Introduction

Supportive services may be defined as organized activities designed to alleviate problems or unfavorable living conditions. An understanding of the existing social service structure is necessary for the coordination or creation of services in any community or region.

Current directories of services detailing both the types and amounts of service available in the community and the characteristics of service clients provide some of this information. However, existing directories are often inadequate for Area Agencies on Aging because they rarely include information on the amount or types of service provided *specifically* to older people. An adequate service plan must include an inventory and analysis of programs specifically available to seniors.

A service analysis is useful in three ways. (1) An inventory provides the investigating agency with a complete data base for understanding the service structure of the community. (2) The analysis of inventory information permits the agency to identify both gaps and overlaps in services, thus allowing the development of an equitable program for the distribution of resources. (3) These inventory and analysis processes promote an understanding and awareness of the needs of seniors, which can be influential in efforts to coordinate services.

Improving the State of the Art

Traditionally, agencies compile lists of services from available directories. Analysis of this data is usually limited to the identification of missing services and comparisons of site location with the areas of elderly population concentrations. The inventory and analysis techniques described in this chapter extend these traditional techniques. A service inventory should identify a wide range of services for older people, senior-specific and non-senior-specific programs, as well as programs provided by informal sources such as clubs, churches, and neighborhood organizations. The inventory should probe service need from several perspectives.

Inventory of Social Services

The service system of a community is viewed as that collection of agencies and organizations whose primary function is to provide social, health, and supportive services. These service providers, such as the city parks department or transit agencies, are labeled as "formal service providers." The service system of a community also includes "informal service providers" such as churches, clubs, friends, family, or others who serve the needs of older people in a less organized manner. Identifying formal service agencies provides a needed base of information for planning. Informal service providers can supplement this base and be especially helpful in reducing gaps in services.

Formal Services

Several steps are involved in the creation of an inventory of formal services:
1. Compiling available data
2. Determining what additional information is needed
3. Deciding on the approach to access this information
4. Designing the instrument
5. Conducting the survey

Compiling available data. To initiate an inventory, readily available information should be collected. General directories in the form of handbooks or computer printouts produced by various agencies serving the area should be analyzed. In the test communities, an initial search turned up three rich sources of already collected service data:
1. A county-wide handbook of social services prepared by the Department of Public Social Services
2. A county-wide inventory of social services prepared by the Council of Government
3. A county-wide computer data base of social services prepared by the United Way

These three sources contained many duplicate entries; however, no single source was complete by itself. Using all available sources enables the planner to compile a master list of agencies who are *potential* senior service providers.

If a list of services is not available, the telephone book can provide a beginning. At the local level, another source of information on service providers are booklets produced by the Chamber of Commerce and other voluntary organizations, such as Rotary, Elks, or Lions. These guidebooks can be particularly helpful as a source of housing services and informal services, especially those offered by churches.

Determining additional data needed. Data from existing handbooks should be analyzed to determine if there are gaps in the following areas:

1. Type of service provided to older people
2. Amount of service provided to older people
3. Characteristics of older people who receive the service (age, sex, race, SES, handicaps, geographic location, means of access)
4. Agency outreach procedures and ability to meet client demand
5. Sources and amounts of funding

Without this information, it is virtually impossible to fully understand the service structure or to identify gaps and overlaps in service. Most service directories do not provide specific information about elderly clients; therefore, a survey is normally required to complete the data.

Deciding on the approach. The survey can be conducted in person, on the telephone, or through the mail. In-person interviews are the most time-consuming but generally the most productive technique. A mail-out survey is easy to conduct but often will result in a low rate of return. Telephone interviews are a good compromise. They can substitute for on-site visits and save time during the interview process. In addition, a response rate of over 90 percent can be expected.

Telephone interviewing, however, does present some problems. It is a good policy to begin with agency directors or administrators, thus insuring a consistent point of view. When directors are unavailable, a number of return calls may be required. Sometimes a less knowledgeable respondent will have to be substituted.

A combination of approaches can also be utilized. For example, after a brief telephone interview a mail-out form to the agency can be used as a supplemental data source. In this case, an initial telephone contact allows the researcher to clarify the purpose of the survey, ask specific key questions, and establish a rapport with agency directors.

Designing the instrument. The instrument should be designed to elicit three types of information: (1) the identification of agencies providing significant service to older people, (2) objective information about the quantity and type of service offered, and (3) historical and descriptive information about the agency itself. Figure 1 illustrates a sample telephone instrument.

The problem of defining senior service providers is somewhat difficult. Clearly, agencies with programs designed primarily for seniors will be included, and programs that have no older participants will be eliminated. There are, however, a number of agencies whose services are not exclusively used by older people. Two criteria should be used to identify significant service providers: (1) the percentage of senior clients to total clients, and (2) the actual number of seniors served per month. These criteria avoid the bias against either large or small organizations while eliminating organizations that reach small numbers of older people and organizations with small elderly proportions to their total client population. The criteria of 20 percent client population and/or 50 older clients are reasonable figures. Thus, Agency A, which provides 75 meals per month to participants over 60, and Agency B, which provides group counseling for 24 people, one-third of which are over 60, would both be included in the formal inventory.

After identifying eligible agencies, preliminary questions should elicit background information about the agency and its programs. Next, questions on type and amount of service and client characteristics should be asked. The name of the service as well as its function should be identified. Units of service should be expressed in terms appropriate to the service type, such as meals/month for nutrition programs, or trips/

Figure 1
Service Inventory Telephone Instrument

Agency Name _____

Address_____

Phone _____

Contact person _____

Title _____

1. In general, what programs or services does your agency provide? _____

_____

2. Do you provide any programs or services which are designed primarily for senior citizens? _____
(If yes, go to page 2. If no, go to next question.)

3. Do any of your programs or services reach some seniors? ____
(If yes, go to next question. If no, end interview.)

4a. What percentage of the people receiving this service are seniors? _____

4b. How many people (of all ages) are served by this program? ____

> *Coding:*
> 1. If yes to question 2 above, (senior specific)
>   —complete interview.
> 2. If less than 20% *and* less than 50 seniors
>   —end interview.
> 3. If more than 20% and less than 50 seniors
>   —complete through Question 7, then end interview.
> 4. If more than 50 seniors
>   —complete interview.

5. Can you tell me a little about the history of your agency (date started, under whose auspices, changes in programs or emphases over the years, etc.)? _____

_____

(Be sure to obtain the date the agency began operations in that community.)

6. Would you describe the programs or services that you provide for seniors?

   a. Service name _____

      Function _____

      Type _____ Units/month_____

   b. Service name _____

      Function _____

      Type _____ Units/month_____

   c. Service name _____

      Function _____

      Type _____ Units/month_____

      Coding for service types:
       1. Information and referral—request units in calls per month.
       2. Transportation—request units in trips per month.
       3. Volunteer (seniors serve as volunteers)—request units in persons per month.
       4. Employment—request units in persons per month.
       5. Health—request units in persons per month.
       6. Counseling—request units in sesions x persons per month.
       7. Nutrition—request units in meals per month.
       8. Recreation—request units in persons per month.
       9. Education—request units in persons per month.
      10. In-home—request units appropriate to type as listed above.

7. Could you describe the characteristics of your senior clients?

   a. age—percent over 75 _____

       percent under 75 _____

   b. racial composition

      _____% White   _____% Black

      _____% Spanish-Speaking   _____% Other

   c. other special characteristics—large percentages of

      below poverty level _____

physically handicapped _____

other_____

(End interview for code 3—more than 20% and less than 50 seniors.)

8. Do you think there are people in the community who need your service but are not using it?   _____

9. How does the demand for your service compare with your ability to provide it?   _____

_____

10. If your budget were increased by 25%, how would you use the additional funds?   _____

_____

(Record response. Code as Administrative, Expand, or New.)

11. What do you feel is the greatest unmet need of seniors in your community (not necessarily a service you would provide)?   ____

_____

12. Do you have specific agreements with other agencies to provide services on a coordinated basis?   _____

(If yes, ask for further information.)   _____

_____

13. To which three agencies do you most frequently refer clients?

_____

14. How is your agency or program funded (Federal, State or local government; donations; fees; United Way; other)?   _____

_____

15. Roughly, how much is your annual budget?   _____

THANK YOU VERY MUCH FOR YOUR TIME

AND INFORMATION

month for transportation programs. Examining client characteristics can locate gaps in service. Distinguishing between the 65–74 and 75+ population as a target group may be important in assessing the adequacy of programs designed for recent retirees, or the frail elderly.

Questions tapping the opinions and perceptions of service providers will serve as indicators of the community's awareness and interest in the needs of seniors. Service demand can be conceived as either perceived demand or actual demand. Perceived service needs can be tapped by asking the agency its perception of what the senior community needs. A question on how the agency would apportion a budget increase provides a measure of organizational behavior. Questions regarding coordination and referral can be helpful in future coordination efforts. Funding sources and budget questions should be placed at the end so that cooperation on other questions will not be jeopardized if this issue proves to be sensitive.

Conducting the survey. Time, personnel, and equipment needed for the survey's completion will depend on the survey method, the size and structure of the community, the level of detail expected, and the resources of the polling agency. Because social service data is so quickly outdated it is important to obtain accurate information within a fairly specific time period. Therefore, a concerted effort conducted over a two-week period is likely to result in more accurate data than a part-time effort conducted over three months.

When telephone or on-site interviews are used, interviewers should be trained in the use of the instrument, and as the survey progresses should meet regularly to review question interpretation. Such collaboration promotes comparability of responses.

Informal Services

Potential informal service providers include church-sponsored groups, clubs, and private local businesses. Several approaches can be used to compile data on these informal service providers. Shops and stores catering to the senior population can be identified as informal service providers.

Clubs and church-sponsored groups, particularly those with well-established programs for seniors, may be identified during the formal service inventory process.

Informal services can be identified by a process similar to that used for formal services. A list of potential providers can be developed through searches of club directories or telephone listings. Useful telephone book headings include churches, clubs, associations, fraternal organizations, and senior citizens organizations. Additional providers may be identified through referrals or contacts with community "knowledgeables" and organizations such as the Chamber of Commerce or the local Council of Churches.

On the survey form, it is sufficient to include only name, address, phone number, type of service provided, and number of seniors served. The telephone interview is the quickest, most effective means of interviewing informal service providers.

Most informal services are limited in scale to a particular neighborhood; therefore, they should be grouped and surveyed according to their location within the community.

Analysis of Data Gained through the Inventory

Compiling the data. After completing the inventory, a list of agencies grouped by service and including address and phone numbers should be prepared. This publication can serve as a directory of services for seniors and as a mailing list for the planning agency. It should be updated yearly to reflect changes in the service system.

The wealth of data should be organized in table form. Figure 2 illustrates how service data can be catalogued. If the number of agencies warrants computerization of the data, coding can be accomplished at this time. Placing the data in table form encourages the analyst to standardize and categorize responses, simplifying further analysis.

Identifying service network developments. A service matrix such as that illustrated in Figure 3 showing agency name, agency affiliation, and service type is a useful guide to understanding the comprehensiveness of the service network. It allows identification of agencies providing multiple services and isolates specific services that are lacking.

Figure 2
Detailed Characteristics of Services Provided

Agency	Area Served	Date Stated	Agency Affiliation	Type of Service	% Seniors	Units of Seniors Served	Age	% Minority	Client Characteristics — Other	Size	25% Increase	Funding
Adult Protective Services	Regional	1975	County	1. Counseling 2. I & R, crisis	75%	50	60+	15%	Below Poverty Level	Small	Expand New—Emergency Hsg	County
American Cancer Society	Regional		National	1. I & R 2. In-home 3. Volunteer 4. Transportation	NK 20% 20% 50%	 20 15 20	57+	min		Large	Expand	United Way, Private
Consumer Action Center	Regional	1974	Local	1. Counseling	10–15%	125				Large	Administration	Community Services Agency
Convalescent Aid Society	Regional	1923	Local	1. In-home	75%	26			Low-income	Small	Not known	Donations
El Centro de Accion Social	Regional	1968	Local	1. I & R	50%	20	55–70	90%	Low-income	Small	Administration Expand	CETA, Donations
FISH	Regional	1963	Local	1. Transportation	75%	600 trips	80+	40%	Low-income	Large	Expand	Volunteer
HEAR Center			Local	1. Health 2. In-home	25% NK	25 NK				Small		
Homemaker Service of Pasadena	Regional	1962	Local	1. In-home	100%	90	75+	20%	Disabled	Small	Administration Reduce fees	Donations, Fees
Jackie Robinson Center	City	1960's	City	1. Health 2. Counseling 3. Recreation 4. Education 5. Volunteer	5% NK NK NK NK	300 NK 200 NK 20	50%–70+	70%	55% poor 5% wheelchair	Large	Administration	City, Federal

Organization	Scope	Established	Level	Services	%	Number	Age	%	Population	Size	Future Plans	Funding
Los Angeles County Senior I & R	City	NK	County	1. I & R	100%	NK	60-75			Small	Administration	CETA
Los Angeles County Military and Veterans			County	1. I & R 2. Counseling	NK	35						County
Los Angeles County Volunteer Services	Regional	1974	County	1. In-home	100%	2200	50% 70+	60%	90% Poor 100% Disabled	Large	New Transportation Legal aid	County, DPSS
Legal Aid Society	Regional		Local	1. Counseling	41%	50			95% Poor	Small	Administrative	United Way, Federal
Meals-on-Wheels	City	1964	Local	1. In-home	100%	2100 meals	75+	10%	Disabled, sick	Large	Not applicable	Fees, Donations
Mental Health Association	Regional	1966	Local	1. Counseling	100%	7	55-65		Women	Small	Administration Expand	United Way, Fees
Pasadena City College	Regional	NK	Comm. Col. District	1. Education	NK					Large	New Nursing homes	Community College District
Pasadena City College Dental Clinic	Regional	1970	Comm. Col. District	1. Health	40%	150				Large	Not applicable	Community College District, Fees
City of Pasadena Recreation Department	City	1976	City	1. Recreation	100%	300				Large	Expand New—Outreach Transportation	City, CETA
Pasadena Lung Association	Regional	NK	Local	1. Health	50%	NK				Large	New Pediatrics	Membership, Donations, AID
Salvation Army	City	1884	National	1. Volunteer 2. Recreation 3. I & R	100% 100% NK	250 58 NK				Large	New—Youth services Emergency housing	Contributions, United Way
Social Security Administration	Regional		Federal	1. I & R	NK							Federal
Villa Park	City	1974	City	1. Transportation 2. Recreation 3. Education 4. I & R 5. Volunteer	100% 100% 100% 100% 100%	120 NK NK 500 NK	50-65	50%		Large	Expand	State, City
Visiting Nurses	Regional	1927	Local	1. In-home	100%	85	75+		Disabled	Small	New—Hospice Education	Fees, Donations

Note: NK = Not Known

If there are many programs for seniors at the city or neighborhood level, the city may have a high level of community awareness and a well-developed senior service system. Few local agencies with senior services may suggest a lack of awareness and a need for educational programs to develop public concern for seniors. If a community has a poorly developed formal service system, the informal system may warrant closer attention.

Examining the history of the network. An analysis of the historical development of senior programs in a community can help to explain the current service network and pinpoint interventions for the planning agency.

The 1960's were generally recognized as a major expansion period for social welfare programs. Cities that expanded social programs during the 1960's gained experience in grantsmanship, agency organization, and administration. These skills benefited the community in the 1970's when funds were made available through the Older Americans Act. Communities which did not develop social programs in the 1960's may lack technical skills and need assistance in grantsmanship or organizational management. Date of agency origin can be a helpful proxy to indicate the agency's experience in program development.

Identifying service needs and service gaps. A hypothetical question which measures the projected behavior of a service agency reads as follows, "If your budget was increased by 25 percent, how would you use the additional funds?"

This question reveals the agency's perception of need in terms of its organization's ability to meet those needs. Responses normally fall within the following three categories:

1. Administrative needs (more staff, more space)
2. Expansion of existing programs (serve more meals per day)
3. New programs or services (e.g., counseling agency would like to provide transportation service)

In addition to isolating services that an older population is likely to need, gaps in services to sub-populations of the elderly should be identified. Services targeted for the 65–74 population as well as the 75+ population should be scrutinized.

Figure 3
Service Matrix Analysis

GENERIC SERVICES

SERVICE AGENCIES	Transportation	Recreation	Education	Info. & Referral	Counseling	Volunteer	Employment	Nutrition	In-Home Service	Health
FEDERAL/STATE AGENCIES										
Military and Veterans Affairs				●	●					
Social Security Administration				●						
COUNTY AGENCIES										
DPSS Adult Protective Services				●	●					
DPSS Homemaker Chore									●	
County Senior Citizens I & R				●						
CITY AGENCIES										
Community Housing Service					●					
Jackie Robinson Center		●	●		●	●				●
Pasadena City College			●							
Recreation Department		●								
Villa Park Center	●	●	●	●	●		●			
NATIONAL ORGANIZATIONS										
American Cancer Society	●			●	●		●		●	
Pasadena Lung Association										●
Salvation Army		●		●	●					
LOCAL ORGANIZATIONS										
Consumer Action Center					●					
Convalescent Aid Society									●	
El Centro de Acción Social				●	●					
HEAR CENTER									●	●
Homemaker Service of Pasadena									●	
Legal Aid Society					●					
Meals-on-Wheels									●	
Mental Health Association					●					
Visiting Nurses Association									●	

The location of a service agency will also influence its use and efficiency. A locational analysis is necessary for identifying service delivery problems in a community. Often service agencies are clustered in downtown areas because of the availability of office space or proximity to other agencies. The accessibility of these services is often directly related to senior residential location or availability of transportation. Locational analysis is particularly important when considering services which are location-bound. Senior centers or recreation and nutrition centers, for example, more often attract people who live within one mile of the site (Tuckman, 1967). Mapping these sites and identifying areas lacking these services helps pinpoint senior populations without adequate access to services.

As illustrated in Figure 4, agency sites should be located on a map of uniform scale and detail. Clear acetate overlays can be used to facilitate locational comparisons. For example, senior centers can be overlayed on transportation routes for evaluating public transporation access to senior centers. Easily distinguished variables include service type or single versus multiple service provider. The geographic area served is often difficult to measure, but is another variable that might be included with this mapping technique.

Residential facilities such as nursing homes and retirement homes should be distinguished from service agencies, and separate locational maps prepared. These two maps will provide a comprehensive overview of services for seniors in the community.

A second series of maps distinguishing specific types of services provided by various agencies is also useful. Each service type should be identified by a different color code to allow the analyst to observe the distribution of any one type of service. Multiservice centers with more than two services, such as illustrated in Figure 5, can be given a special designation to facilitate analysis.

These maps display in an easily readable form agencies in geographic proximity that provide similar services, and may suggest opportunities for coordination. The combination of population density maps with service locations will identify spatial service gaps.

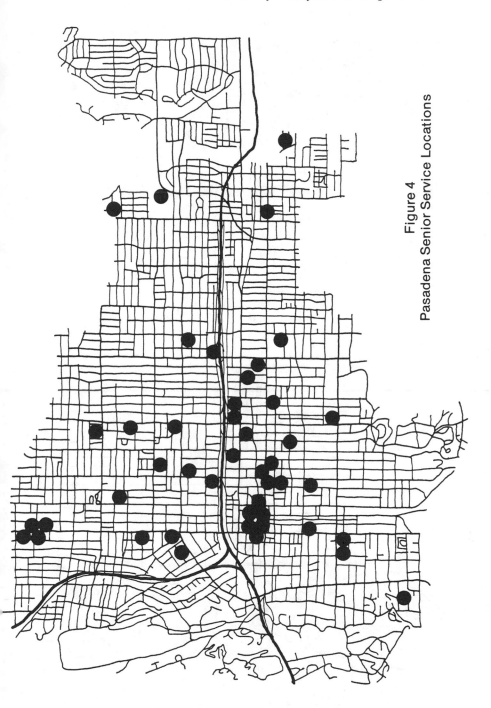

Figure 4
Pasadena Senior Service Locations

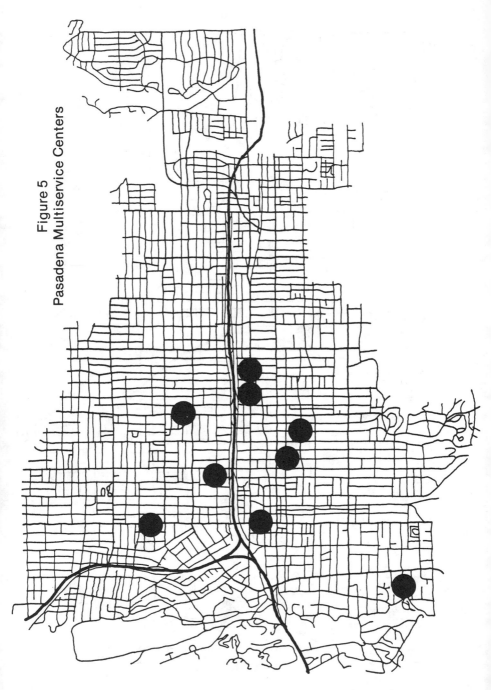

Figure 5
Pasadena Multiservice Centers

Coordinating Services

Coordination can be used to fill gaps in service or to eliminate inefficient service duplication. Certain programs such as health and counseling are usually open to all age groups, although seniors compose a significant proportion of their clientele. Assuming that the health and counseling needs of older people differ from other age groups, a coordinated effort among existing providers to initiate a program tailored to the needs of older people would be appropriate. The special needs of minority or handicapped elderly might be met in a similar fashion.

Coordination can also mean linking people to services through an information system, referrals, or centralized services. A major service delivery problem involves increasing the awareness of the older resident to the availability of programs. Outreach efforts are one means of providing this link. When outreach is limited, the agency is often not able to attract new clients. Coordination can insure that outreach efforts will involve new needy participants. The development of interagency agreements for referrals from one service provider to another can be a good solution. Service planners could use information provided by the service inventory to target specific agencies for coordination and thus improve seniors' access to services.

Findings and Recommendations

1. *The service network of a community will not necessarily reflect the demographic characteristics of that community.* Total population, population of seniors, percentage of population over age 65, density of senior population, and percentage of senior population below the poverty level are characteristics used to suggest the need for services, but do not indicate how well needs are being met. Service planning should involve more than examination of demographic characteristics. It should consider the array of existing services and historical trends in the development of a service structure.

2. *Existing directories of service agencies are usually inadequate for planning, coordinating, and implementing*

senior services. A service inventory of senior service providers and the compilation of information on the amount and type of service given will provide a base of information. Analysis of this data will highlight needed interventions.

3. *Lack of experience can restrict a community's development of new services.* Service planners may be able to provide information on sources of funding or technical assistance in grant writing to communities with an underdeveloped service structure.

4. *Local or grassroots organizations are important in developing a community's service network.* Available federal and county services do not vary widely between communities. City and local organizations are the major source for extensive program development in a community. Service planners should stimulate local initiative by involving community organizations in senior problems.

5. *Informal service providers can fill gaps in the formal service network.* Informal service providers should be encouraged to become formal service agencies in communities where there are large service gaps.

6. *Some programs tend to be senior-specific.* While there are nutrition and volunteer programs geared for the senior population, there is a lack of other services, such as health and counseling, that are senior-specific. Assuming that senior needs may differ, service providers might encourage existing providers of these services to develop special programs for seniors.

7. *There is a link between outreach and demand for service.* Because agencies control the demand of their service by controlling their outreach efforts, agencies reach only the population already aware of services. These seniors may not be the ones most in need of services. Service planners might provide a centralized outreach service so that each agency does not completely control its own demand. Such a service may reach more potential service recipients.

Summary

The methods outlined above focus on the collection of information through a service inventory and the analysis of this data using locational techniques, charts, and matrices. An inventory of formal and informal service provides the planning agency with a data base which can be helpful in understanding the complexity and interrelationships of a community's service structure. A telephone survey is a successful means of obtaining comprehensive information in a timely fashion. The addition of informal services to a compilation of formal services adds depth and may be particularly important when planning for small target areas.

In analyzing inventory data, the planning agency should be able to identify gaps in services and understand the community's interest in and awareness of senior service needs. Mapping is useful in identifying areas of the community which are under-served, particularly by "location-bound" services. Charts and tables can be used to identify particular client groups not being served and uneven distributions of service. Armed with a detailed understanding of the community's social service network, service planners can make intelligent choices in expanding and developing a balanced, efficient system.

References

Tuckman, J. Factors related to attendance in a center for older people. *Journal of the American Geriatrics Society,* 1967, *15*(5), 475.

6

TRANSPORTATION SYSTEM ANALYSIS TECHNIQUES

six

Sherman Gordon
and Keith Shirasawa

Sherman Gordon is a Ph.D. graduate student in the Urban and Regional Planning program and a Research Assistant on the Administration on Aging funded Community Analysis Techniques research grant, Environmental Studies Laboratory, Andrus Gerontology Center, University of Southern California, Los Angeles, California.

Keith Shirasawa is a Planner with Gerontological Planning Associates, Santa Monica, California.

Introduction

Transportation is a key link providing access to goods, services, friends, and relatives. Transportation can be public or private, vehicular or pedestrian. Transportation systems can be expensive and complex, such as freeway networks or computer-operated bus networks, or simple and low-cost, such as pedestrian sidewalks. No matter how simple or complex the system, the availability of transportation does not insure mobility. If there are barriers to the use of a system, the mobility of particular user groups may not be maximized. Constant monitoring of transportation systems is necessary to insure increased mobility for older people.

In planning transportation systems, the elderly can be viewed as a special group because their trip needs are different. They make fewer work trips; they are more dependent on public transportation, and may have physical limitations that complicate access. No other group suffers more from transportation barriers. Bus design and bus schedules are often inappropriate, driving an automobile can be expensive and confusing, and even walking can present hazards. There is considerable evidence that elderly mobility is greatly affected by transportation systems inappropriate for their needs (Gillan & Wachs[1], 1976).

Improving the State of the Art

The quantity and quality of data on existing transportation systems varies from city to city and system to system. Although there is usually good information on existing bus networks, data on pedestrian activity and improvements is almost universally nonexistent.

Recommendations for improvements in the existing transportation network will focus on bus, automobile, dial-a-ride, and pedestrianism. The conventional *bus* carries many elderly, but barriers such as inappropriate routing, high fares, poor bus design, driver courtesy, and perceived crime limit its use. The private *automobile* provides transportation for a majority of the elderly in most urban areas, with the primary limiting factors being cost and the driving environment. Special transportation systems such as *dial-a-ride* are used to supplement the bus for special kinds of trips and for frail users. *Pedestrianism* accounts for most short trips and is important in longer trips since walking is involved to and from all other modes of transit. No one system serves more than a portion of all elderly trip needs, although the automobile is the most extensively used mode.

Analysis Techniques

This section will detail three methodologies which can be used to analyze, plan, and implement needed transportation changes and/or improvements. A *bus service analysis* will measure the coverage of the existing bus service network. Comparisons of this network can be made with elderly residential distributions to locate pockets of under-served elderly.

A *trip survey* questionnaire can yield excellent information on elderly trip-making, bus design, and driver courtesy problems. Although it can be expensive and time-consuming, its costs may be defrayed by other agencies.

Zone matrix analysis is a means of identifying elderly transportation pathways. It identifies heavily used routes which can be targeted for increased bus service and improvements in the driving environment.

Bus Service Analysis

This method combines the geographic distribution and service attributes of bus service. Two variables are used to classify the suitability of bus service: (1) the walking distance to a bus stop, and (2) the waiting time at the bus stop.[2] Three blocks was assumed as the maximum distance most seniors are willing to walk to a bus stop. While seniors may be willing to wait for a bus longer than are younger age cohorts, one hour is the functional maximum. Using bus stop locations and frequency of service data, the system can be analyzed in a similar manner to the Glendale system illustrated in Figure 1.

1. Local bus routes are first drawn on a map of the urban area.

Figure 1
Glendale Bus Service Analysis

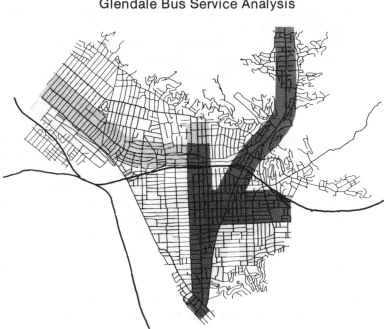

Average Headway (minutes)

■ 15 min.

☐ 16–30 min.

☐ 30 + min.

Note: Three block radius from bus stop defines access corridor.

Source: Southern California Rapid Transit District (SCRTD).

2. A three block radius is drawn around each bus stop.

3. Each area is shaded using colors to represent the frequency of service along that bus route (15 minutes or less, 16 to 30 minutes, and 31 minutes or more).

4. A map of the 60+ population density is also drawn.

5. Finally, the two maps are compared to identify significant senior population concentrations which are underserved by the existing bus network.

Once identified, underserved areas can become target areas for new routing or increased frequency of service. With this information, local bus companies can be approached about needed changes.

Bus routes and schedules used in this simple and quick analysis of service can be easily obtained. Elderly population (60+) by census tract is available for all metropolitan areas.

Trip Survey

A trip survey can be used to identify the type and scale of unsatisfied elderly transportation needs. A trip survey usually includes information such as origin, destination, trip purpose, frequency and time of travel, mode of transportation, problems with existing transportation, and desire for increased travel. Descriptive demographic data such as age and income are also desirable in order to identify specific improvements for particular users.

Type of survey. The survey instrument may be administered in different ways. A face-to-face personal interview method is an expensive and time-consuming survey procedure, but the return rate is high and the answers reliable. A handout/mail-back questionnaire is inexpensive and quicker to administer; however, the return rate may be low, causing sample reliability to suffer. A comprehensive procedure is the supervised questionnaire, completed and returned immediately. It can be administered to a group of people such as bus passengers or shopping center patrons with a staff member present to answer questions. Utilizing this method, the answers are reliable, the return rate high, and the cost moderate.

Figure 2 provides an example of a typical instrument. Simple language and large size lettering should be used for ease of reading and interpretation, and the instrument should take no longer than 5 to 7 minutes to administer. Avoid hypothetical questions such as, "What would you do if . . . ?" Carefully word sensitive questions such as those relating to income or occupation. Finally, keep questions in a logical sequence.[3]

Figure 2
Passenger Survey Instrument

PASSENGER SURVEY

The RTD is surveying passengers on this bus line in order to find out what your transit needs are and how we can best respond to your needs. All replies are completely confidential, so please answer all the questions as accurately as possible. Thank you for your help.

PLEASE ANSWER ALL THE QUESTIONS AND RETURN THIS FORM TO THE RTD REPRESENTATIVE

1. Where did you start this trip? (Indicate nearest street intersection)

   _____ and _____
   (Major Street)   (Nearest Cross-Street)

2. Where are you going? (Indicate nearest street intersection)

   _____ and _____
   (Major Street)   (Nearest Cross-Street)

3. How did you get to *this bus*?
   - Drove ☐
   - Walked ☐
   - Was Driven ☐
   - Other _____ (PLEASE SPECIFY)
   - Transferred from bus line number _____ (SPECIFY)

4. Where did you get on *this bus*? (Indicate nearest street intersection)

   _____ and _____
   (Major Street)   (Nearest Cross-Street)

5. Where will you get off *this bus*? (Indicate nearest street intersection)

   _____ and _____
   (Major Street)   (Nearest Cross-Street)

6. After you get off this bus, you will:
   - Drive ☐
   - Walk ☐
   - Be Driven ☐
   - Other _____ (PLEASE SPECIFY)
   - Transfer to bus line number _____ (SPECIFY)

7. How many days a week do you usually ride the bus?
   - Five or more ☐
   - Four ☐
   - Three ☐
   - Two ☐
   - One ☐
   - Less Than One ☐

8. What is the purpose of this trip? (Check one)
   - Work ☐
   - School ☐
   - Social/Recreational ☐
   - Shopping ☐
   - Medical ☐
   - Other _____ (PLEASE SPECIFY)

9. What type of fare did you pay to get on this bus?
   - Cash Fare of _____ ¢ (Specify Amount)
   - Used a Transfer ☐
   - $18 Monthly Pass ☐
   - Monthly Pass with Express Stamp ☐
   - $12 Student Pass ☐
   - $4 Senior Citizen Pass ☐
   - $4 Handicapped Pass ☐
   - Other _____ (PLEASE SPECIFY)

10. What is your home address?

Number	Street	Apartment Number	City	Zip Code

11. You are: Male ☐   Female ☐

12. What is your age? _____ (PLEASE SPECIFY)

13. How many automobiles in running condition are there in your household?
    - No Cars ☐
    - One Car ☐
    - Two Cars ☐
    - Three or more Cars ☐

14. Please indicate the number of persons in each age group who live in your household. (Include yourself)
    - Under 18 _____
    - 18-29 _____
    - 30-39 _____
    - 40-49 _____
    - 50-61 _____
    - 62 and over _____

15. What is the total annual income of your household?
    - Under $5000 ☐
    - $5,000 to $9,999 ☐
    - $10,000 to $14,999 ☐
    - $15,000 to $19,999 ☐
    - $20,000 to $24,999 ☐
    - $25,000 and over ☐

16. Do you have any physical handicaps which make it difficult for you to get to or use the bus?
    Yes ☐   No ☐

17. What is the main reason you ride the bus?
    - No car available ☐
    - Prefer bus to driving ☐
    - Bus is economical ☐
    - Bus is convenient ☐
    - Other _____ (PLEASE SPECIFY)

18. How would you rate RTD as an agency providing public transportation?
    - Excellent ☐
    - Good ☐
    - Fair ☐
    - Poor ☐

PLEASE USE THE SPACE BELOW FOR COMMENTS OR SUGGESTIONS:

N° 1782   THANK YOU FOR YOUR HELP. BE SURE TO RETURN THIS FORM TO THE RTD REPRESENTATIVE BEFORE YOU LEAVE THE BUS.

RTD 425 S. MAIN
Los Angeles
90013

Source: Southern California Rapid Transit District (SCRTD).

Zone Matrix Analysis

The zone matrix technique is a method used to analyze elderly trip patterns by identifying routes that are the most heavily traveled. With this information, existing bus routes can be compared to elderly trip patterns to identify gaps in service, and heavily traveled routes can be targeted for bus design improvements or environmental improvements to aid the elderly driver and pedestrian.

The first step is to divide an urban area into several analysis zones. Small urban areas can be divided into 6 to 10 zones (each containing approximately 20 to 40 blocks), while larger areas may require 20 or more. Zones should be designated logically around major activity centers. Widely differing land uses, such as industrial and residential, should be included in separate zones. Transportation zones should coincide with other data boundaries such as census tracts wherever possible.

If a trip survey is utilized, this data specifying trip origins and destinations can be plotted. In place of empirical data one can obtain approximations by plotting trip generators (hospitals or shopping centers) and comparing these with elderly residential concentrations. Proxy data such as this can be useful in updating existing origin-destination data, but by itself may be somewhat unreliable for initial routing decisions.

After zones have been defined and origin-destination data collected, the number of trips beginning and ending in each zone can be calculated. The number of trips from each zone to other zones are computed. The analysis facilitates the identification of densely traveled routes. The zone matrix illustrated in Figure 3 suggests several trip patterns. The 50 round trips per day that begin and end in Zone E indicate the need for a loop or circulating service within that zone. The 45 round trips per day that go between Zone C and Zone E suggest the need for a regularly scheduled bus service. The lower trip densities in other zones indicate dispersed origins and destinations where dial-a-ride may be most appropriate. A zone matrix analysis allows comparisons between elderly trip patterns and service offered and identifies target routes for improving existing transit, automobile use, and pedestrian safety.

Figure 3
Origin/Destination Matrix Analysis[1]

Destination (Zones to): / Origin (Zones from):	Zone A	Zone B	Zone C	Zone D	Zone E	Total Trip Origins	% of Total Trip Origins
Zone A	15	20	25	0	0	50	17%
Zone B	25	10	15	0	0	50	17%
Zone C	10	10	25	5	45	95	31%
Zone D	0	0	5	25	20	50	17%
Zone E	0	0	0	5	50	55	18%
Total Trip Destinations	40	40	70	35	115	300	100%
% of Total Destinations	13%	13%	24%	12%	38%	100%	

[1]Assumes all trips return to zone of origination. In order to arrive at the total number of one-way trips, the above numbers must be doubled.

Source: Institute for Public Administration, 1975.

Bus Improvement Options

The standard 50-passenger bus is the most common component of public transportation in the United States and serves the greatest number of elderly. In most urban areas service appears to be adequate, the ride comfortable, and the fare reasonable. However, the majority of elderly do not ride the bus or are limited in their use of buses. Improvements are needed if the bus is to realize its potential contribution to elderly mobility.

Increased frequency of service and expanded routes. These two improvements are the most common attempts to make the bus more attractive. Some urban areas do indeed have such inadequate bus service that increased frequency and expanded routes are required to bring service up to a minimum level of acceptability. Although shorter walking distances to bus stops and shorter headways between buses to encourage patronage from younger age groups, the elderly do not increase ridership when routing or frequency of service is increased beyond a minimum level. Increases in routing and frequency are expensive; therefore, other improvements which may have a greater impact on elderly patronage should be considered. Each urban area should be examined using the bus route analysis and zone matrix analysis to see if existing services are adequate.[4]

Reduced fares. Senior discounts are available in most bus systems throughout the country. Reductions normally range from 10 to 100 percent, but are most commonly set at 50 percent. Numerous empirical studies have found that elderly patronage is not significantly effected by fare reductions (Kraft & Domencich, 1968; Kemp, 1973; Mullen, 1975). Although patronage may not be increased, a good rationale for fare reductions is as an income supplement for low income seniors. There is a high probability that only current patrons will benefit from fare reductions.

Bus design. Changes in bus design are increasingly recognized as having significant impact on elderly patronage. Trip surveys have documented elderly dissatisfaction with existing vehicles. Elderly who ride the bus regularly and elderly who do not ride buses are dissatisfied with vehicle design. Specific complaints concern the lack of storage space for packages, poor lighting, steep and narrow steps, slippery floor surfaces, poor access to the door, and lack of provisions for the handicapped. Some changes are expensive to implement; many, such as easy access, may require new vehicles— "kneeling buses." However, some changes, such as nonslip floors and improved lighting, are easy to implement.

The information needed to alter bus design can be

gathered through existing guidelines and local surveys. Most vehicle-design guidelines and elderly passenger requirements have general applicability.[5] Specific survey information is required to prioritize needed changes. Trip surveys can be used to note deficiencies. Needed local design changes can be identified, including those which remove barriers and thus attract new elderly riders.

Driver courtesy and sensitivity. Elderly often complain about driver courtesy. Drivers are often impatient with elderly persons who may take extra time boarding and may ask questions about destinations, transfers, and fares. Training drivers to improve attitudes is a relatively simple process which can improve the older person's attitude toward the bus system. Information can be gathered through trip surveys, along with the information on bus design changes. Survey data can be used to identify problem drivers and design a sensitizing educational program.

Perceived threat of crime. The crime problem is often overlooked as an improvement to the transportation system, although no other change would do more to increase elderly bus patronage. Many older people are afraid to walk to bus stops, wait for a bus, or ride the bus. Trip survey data can reveal these concerns and can also identify troublesome routes. Once identified, improvements are difficult to implement; however, if elderly mobility is to be maximized, crime fears must be reduced.

Automobile Improvement Options

Despite the evidence that a majority of elderly are auto-dependent and not transit-dependent (Wachs & Gillan, 1976; Paaswell & Edelstein, 1976)[6], efforts to improve the elderly driving environment have been exceedingly limited. Suggestions about improving elderly automobile mobility have come primarily from organization such as NRTA/AARP or the American Automobile Association.

Lighting, sign, and lane improvements. These improvements can make it easier for the elderly to travel by automobile. Signs should have larger lettering, greater figure-to-ground contrast, and be positioned to avoid other overhead signs. Traffic lights should have greater color contrast and should be placed in uniform positions. Residential streets should be better lighted, especially around parked cars. Traffic lanes should be marked with fluorescent paint and reflectors, and left-turn lane arrows added. Suggestions such as these can be introduced by service planners, particularly when public works improvements are slotted for neighborhood areas with high concentrations of elderly. Trip survey data can specify elderly trip origins and destinations, and can pinpoint streets elderly drivers use regularly, so limited funds can be effectively used. Corridors of heavy elderly traffic can be identified using the previously determined zone matrix analysis; thus, major thoroughfares within the corridors can be targeted for improvement.

Drivers' education. Older people face two significant problems in driving: (1) the decline of individual driving skills; and (2) the increasing complexity of the driving environment. The National Safety Council has launched the first major effort to teach elderly drivers new coping skills to alleviate common fears. This program concentrates on defensive driving techniques, automobile maintenance, and advance trip planning, while stressing the use of familiar routes and the avoidance of rush hour traffic (Waddell, 1976). Courses such as these should be publicized at locations older drivers are likely to frequent. Some of these locations would be senior centers, shopping centers, hospitals, and the State Department of Motor Vehicles. Traffic court also can assign elderly individuals to classes in response to traffic violations.

Trip surveys may contain some information about problems elderly drivers experience—lighting, signs, and dangerous intersections. Accident data collected by police or traffic engineering departments can also pinpoint problem locations. Local problem areas should be included in a comprehensive educational program.

Priority parking. Overcrowded parking lots can deter elderly drivers. Major elderly destinations are obvious targets for such a program. Police departments may express concern about the enforcement of preferred senior parking or its effect on overall vehicle parking in the city. The planning agency should consider solutions such as parking stickers and weigh the benefits of increased elderly mobility against enforcement problems.

Information specifying locations for preferred parking can be obtained from trip surveys. Interviews with supervisorial personnel at common elderly destinations can estimate the number of elderly clients who arrive by automobile.

Maintenance and repair discount programs. These kinds of programs have ample precedent in drug stores, supermarkets, and other retail outlets which offer discount goods and services to the elderly. The high cost of new cars encourages many elderly to maintain older automobiles. Maintenance and repair costs thus represent a significant outlay of funds for the elderly. Discount programs can benefit senior mobility by providing more reliable automobiles. To institute such a program, service planners should identify the stations appropriate for discount programs. Census data can be used in combination with the location of automobile service providers to establish locations. A major selling point of a senior discount program is the benefit to the service station's community image and a possible increase in net income due to increased patronage.

Dial-a-ride Improvement Options

Dial-a-ride is one member of a newly developed transportation option called "paratransit." Paratransit modes typically provide specialized transportation supplements to the conventional public transit system. Their basic advantage is a high level of service. Additionally, they can more efficiently reach low density areas which are currently underserviced by conventional public transportation.

Dial-a-ride offers transportation in small to medium-sized vehicles ranging from automobiles to 15-passenger vans. Dial-a-ride service often provides door-to-door convenience, thus avoiding the danger and inconvenience of walking in unfriendly neighborhoods, waiting at bus stops, or driving in traffic. These vehicles offer a comfortable ride, ample storage space for packages, and easier access for the frail or handicapped.

Dial-a-ride is one of the most appropriate transportation alternatives for the elderly. However, these systems are expensive because of high operating costs and often must be subsidized. If demand is low, the subsidy required may be substantial. Demand depends on many factors, but the easiest and best predictor is population density. Empirical evaluation of existing dial-a-ride systems (Kirby, et al., 1974) suggest that ideal demand densities range between 4,000 and 8,000 individuals per square mile. Densities lower than 2,000 individuals per square mile will not generate sufficient demand, and densities of above 8,000 individuals per square mile may overload the system. In addition to density, other predictors include auto availability, client income, number of frail/handicapped users, and location of common trip destinations. Data on these variables may be more difficult to obtain than those on density.

Careless planning can lead to a costly and unserviceable system. Communities which have thoughtlessly implemented these expensive systems without sufficient planning have lost considerable amounts of money. The following critical issues should be addressed in the design of a dial-a-ride system: (1) overall feasibility of the geographic area under consideration, (2) economic feasibility of a senior-only system, and (3) adequacy of demand for an instantaneous response (as opposed to reservation) system.

Major questions that should be raised in the planning of a dial-a-ride system for the elderly include the following.

1. *Is the density of the general population within the acceptable range for dial-a-ride?* The normal feasibility range for a dial-a-ride falls within the 2,000–8,000 individuals per square mile range. Many inner-city elderly live in areas with densities that range up to 25,000 people per square mile. In such areas, dial-a-ride should be designed as a supplement to normal bus service, and may be especially useful at night and on weekends when demand falls and congestion is reduced. Suburban elderly normally live in areas of less than 1,000 people per square mile. These outlying areas cannot be economically serviced by conventional public transit; thus, dial-a-ride represents the only viable public transit option available to this growing population segment.[7] Efficient provision of

service requires dial-a-ride to be limited in such areas. Possible limitations include 24-hour advance reservations, eliminating night and weekend service, and limiting destinations and service area to avoid long trips.

2. *Are there enough seniors living at sufficient densities to support a senior-only dial-a-ride system?* Since senior demand for public transportation is about the same as that of the general population, densities required for a general dial-a-ride service should also be in the 2,000 to 8,000 per square mile range. Senior-only dial-a-ride is especially feasible if densities are in the middle 4,000–6,000 per square mile range. Growing numbers of suburban elderly living at densities of less than 250 per square mile cannot be feasibly serviced by a senior-only dial-a-ride. Mobility for these individuals can be improved only if the system is opened to the general population.

Communities may have the same percentage of elderly population but quite different elderly densities. Figure 4 illustrates the two target cities, each containing a similar distribution of 60+ population. In Glendale, 15 out of 24 census tracts are within the 2,000–8,000 people per square mile density, while Pasadena has adequate senior densities in only six out of 30 census tracts. Although these two communities have the same percentage of elderly population, Glendale could operate dial-a-ride efficiently while Pasadena could not.

3. *Should dial-a-ride be demand-responsive (average 20-minute delay from phone call to pickup) or reservation-only (24 hours advance notice)?* Instantaneous response provides excellent service at high cost, while a reservation-only system sacrifices high service for a lower cost. An instantaneous response system often requires sophisticated dispatching equipment, while a reservation-only system normally will not. Demand-responsive systems often carry passengers to dispersed destinations from widely-separated origins; therefore, a predictable demand must be established to maximize vehicle usage. A reservation system enables origins and destinations to be coordinated in advance; thus total miles traveled and costs are reduced. The key determining factor is density. Densities in the range of 4,000 to 6,000 people per square mile can easily support demand-responsive systems. A low

Figure 4
Demand Response Elderly Population Densities

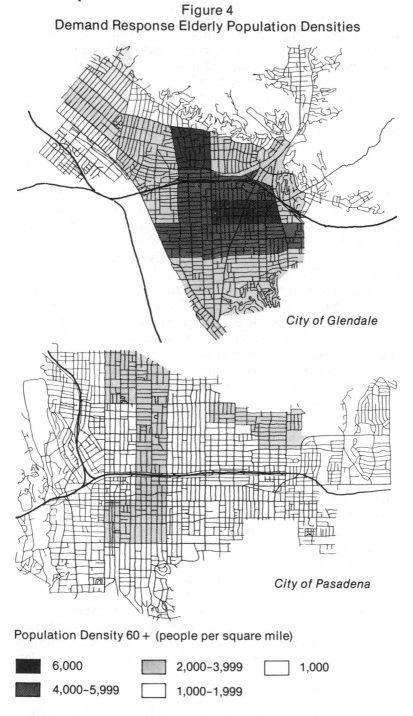

City of Glendale

City of Pasadena

Population Density 60 + (people per square mile)

■ 6,000		▦ 2,000–3,999		□ 1,000	
▨ 4,000–5,999		□ 1,000–1,999			

marginal density of 2,000 to 3,000 people per square mile usually can support only a reservation system.

In marginal situations a combination of systems might be possible. High-density areas could use a reservation-only dial-a-ride to supplement fixed-line bus service during weekdays, with demand-responsive dial-a-ride taking over at night and on weekends. Suburban low-density situations could support demand-responsive dial-a-ride during weekdays and reservation-only dial-a-ride during lower demand evenings and weekends. Whatever combination is chosen, the system forms should be matched to demand levels, with service quality balanced against system costs.

4. *What service area should dial-a-ride cover?* Empirical studies (Kirby, et al., 1974) have concluded that dial-a-ride systems should cover areas of approximately 6 to 20 square miles in size. Larger areas necessitate long trips, which are extremely costly, while smaller areas may not yield enough patronage to support a system. The shape of the service area and the location of goods and services within the area are important. Elongated areas or areas of dispersed destinations are expensive to service because trip lengths may be considerable. Thus, service areas should be designated utilizing origin-destination patterns. The service area should include only census tracts with densities in the 2,000 to 8,000 individuals per square mile range. Multiple service designations should be considered when target areas are larger than 20 square miles.

5. *What types of trips should the dial-a-ride system serve?* Each trip type has a unique cost profile. Trips involving several individuals traveling from the same origin to the same destination are less expensive than trips carrying the same number of individuals from separate origins to separate destinations. The precarious financial status of a dial-a-ride system requires consideration of the kinds of trips made. There are four basic trip types a dial-a-ride system can service.

The *many-to-many* trip involves picking up riders at dispersed origins and delivering them to dispersed destinations. Such multiple origins and destinations require a high number of miles driven for a given number of individuals. The gap between revenue generated and vehicle operating costs is greatest for this type of trip. Unfortunately, this is perhaps the most common trip older people make in urban areas.

Many-to-few trips involve picking up riders at dispersed residential origins and taking them to a few fixed destinations. Costs are reduced for transporting a given number of individuals, since the total number of miles traveled is reduced by limiting destination alternatives. The operating deficit is less than that of the previous type because revenue per vehicle mile is substantially increased. Trips to hospitals, major shopping centers, and downtown are examples of this trip type.

Few-to-few trips involve picking up riders at a limited number of origins (housing for the elderly, apartment houses, social service agencies, or shopping centers) and transporting them to a limited number of destinations (hospitals, other social service agencies, or cultural centers). These trips are low-cost and often can be scheduled on a regular basis. Revenue per vehicle hour is high because pick-up and delivery time is reduced and vehicles can be scheduled in advance. These trips rarely create operating deficits.

One-to-one trips involve picking up riders at a single origin, often a congregate housing site or multipurpose senior center, and transporting them to a single destination, usually a recreation or cultural center. Miles traveled for a given number of individuals are minimized and revenue per vehicle hour maximized. Such group trips can be scheduled in advance and in slack demand periods.

Dial-a-ride efficiency can be maximized by scheduling one-to-one trips, while service can be maximized by emphasizing many-to-many trips. Ideally, operating deficits can be held down by scheduling many-to-many trips at night, on weekends, and during other non-peak hours when fixed-route systems are not operating. Information about the number and frequency of such trip types can be obtained from trip survey data which provide information about origins, destinations, time, and frequency of travel.

Pedestrian Improvement Options

Perhaps the most significant but yet overlooked alternative to improving mobility is to facilitate and encourage pedestrian movement. While the elderly are not unique in their reliance on pedestrianism for mobility, they constitute a disproportionately large number of this nation's pedestrian fatalities. The elderly, who represent 10 percent of the population, account for 25 percent of the total number of pedestrian deaths in the nation (National Safety Council, 1967). Many older people find themselves spending more and more time as pedestrians because walking represents the only means to reach neighborhood-level goods and services.

Despite the dependence of many seniors on pedestrianism and the number of older people who are killed in accidents as pedestrians, service planners rarely consider improvements in the pedestrian environment. Unfortunately, most traffic engineering departments also ignore the needs of pedestrians, despite the fact that they are responsible for moving *both* pedestrian and vehicular traffic.

Service planners face several problems when dealing with pedestrian issues. First, the information available to deal with these problems is hard to gather. Time constraints and limited staff resources also complicate the situation. Service planners need not be technical experts in this area. However, they have a responsibility to advocate for older pedestrians with public works officials.

Accessing existing information sources. There is normally little empirical information available detailing how pedestrians use environments. It is unusual to find a traffic circulation element of a general plan that details the needs and special problems of pedestrians, regardless of age. When problems of older pedestrians are mentioned, they are almost always assumed to be similar to those of the handicapped.

Traffic engineering departments are responsible for collecting and maintaining pedestrian data; however, the means of collecting and storing such information is not standardized between cities. While some traffic departments maintain computer records of accidents involving older pedestrians, others rely totally on police reports. Similarly, there is no uniform method of documenting the streets most heavily utilized by pedestrians.

Where pedestrian data is available, the following questions should be tested:

1. Is the data detailing the number of pedestrian-vehicular conflicts available by age cohorts and aggregated by intersection or location?[8]

2. Are special considerations given or allowances made for older pedestrians?[9]

3. Which intersections are more often crossed by older people?

Just as there exists no standardized recordkeeping method among agencies, the responses to pedestrian problems can vary widely. Some cities regularly send a staff person into the field to make observations whenever a change is suggested to determine if the proposed solution is appropriate. Other cities may follow standard formulas without exception.[10] One would not expect to have *every* light paced for older people, however, compromises may be obtained.

The service planner should note the sensitivity with which a traffic engineering department both conceptualizes and responds to the special needs of older pedestrians. Although most traffic engineers are charged with providing for the fast and safe flow of vehicular traffic, individual attitudes can be more significant than official policies in making adjustments for pedestrians.

Other data sources. One obvious source of additional data is police accident records. Many police departments, however, are reluctant to share their records because of confidentiality considerations. Emergency room admission records, if readily accessible and translatable, can be another potential surrogate measure.

The local office of the Automobile Association of America or the National Automobile Club can provide guidance to accessible accident data; however, it will most likely be aggregated on a citywide scale, giving it marginal utility in designing neighborhood level interventions.

Analysis of existing data sources. Locating accidents involving older pedestrians on a scaled map of the neighborhood will pinpoint paths and intersections that pose a particular danger to older people. A temporal analysis of accident times can identify when accidents involving pedestrians occur most frequently. A map combining both variables will detail both *when* and *where* accidents involving pedestrians occur frequently.

Types of accidents should also be noted. Educational or training programs can be helpful in reducing accidents involving jaywalking. Simple "hardware" solutions, such as stop signs, signals, and crosswalks are also available. The specific nature of improvements normally remains the decision of the traffic engineering department. However, a service planner with information about where, when, and how the problem occurs should be able to suggest the most appropriate intervention.

Traffic engineering departments are often the sole source of pedestrian data, thus allowing the planner to quickly determine its availability. Many departments, however, may have little if any interest in accommodating older pedestrians.

A constructive, non-threatening approach may result in the identification of problem areas, perhaps in the course of a brief telephone conversation. This approach is contingent on providing the engineer with a *specific* statement of the desired information. Familiarity with the available data is necessary in order to make the most appropriate suggestions and interventions to traffic engineering and public works departments.

Interventions in the pedestrian-scale environment. A number of interventions can be employed to improve the quality of the pedestrian environment for older community residents. The following briefly describe several options along with the type of information needed to determine the appropriateness of each intervention:

1. *"Hardware" improvements.* This option includes installation of traffic lights, stop signs, and other signalling devices, and is the most common approach used by traffic engineering departments. Hardware improvements are generally based on the volume of vehicular traffic flowing through a particular intersection. Devices are also placed at intersections with a history of pedestrian/vehicular conflicts. Community groups may directly request the installation of a stop sign at a dangerous intersection in the neighborhood.

2. *Educational programs.* This alternative places responsibility for safety with the pedestrian. Educational programs inform older pedestrians about measures they can take to avoid accidents. Training is most appropriate if accident data demonstrates that a number of accidents are caused by care-

lessness or ignorance. Information on type of pedestrian accidents is necessary to determine the utility of such a program.

3. *Non-signaling hardware improvements.* Included in this category are marked crosswalks, street lights, and other improvements provided for convenience rather than for control. Areas that generate large volumes of pedestrian traffic, such as shopping centers and schools, usually have these improvements. However, many traffic engineers are particularly reluctant to install crosswalks because they feel such improvements give the pedestrian a false sense of security.

The most appropriate intervention to a particular pedestrian problem remains the decision of the traffic engineer. However, a service planner who is aware of the options and interventions available may provide constructive input to the traffic engineer.

Summary

The primary data generated from a trip survey questionnaire are extremely helpful in understanding transportation alternatives. A trip survey is difficult to design, expensive and time-consuming to administer and analyze. No other technique, however, can yield information which approaches the depth and quality of a well-managed trip survey. It can help in every phase of improving elderly mobility, from vehicle design to improving pedestrian safety. There are quicker means of acquiring elderly trip data, such as traffic generators or agency interviews, but the wide utility of the trip survey may normally make it cost effective.

The two primary attempts to improve the attractiveness of the *bus* to the elderly have been: (1) increasing service routing and frequency, and (2) offering reduced fares. Past analyses suggest that elderly trip demand responds more to service than cost. Thus, reducing fares alone may not increase ridership.

The importance of planning implementable transportation improvements can be exemplified by the use of paratransit alternatives such as a dial-a-ride. Because public agencies with little transportation experience often fail to gather basic information about elderly origin-destination patterns before designing the system, many dial-a-ride systems have failed shortly after implementation. Surviving systems often operate only with the help of enormous subsidies, the need for which has increased in recent years. Inadequate planning can create a system that offers the wrong service with inappropriate vehicles during the wrong time.

Implications

Transportation improvements normally take place categorically with little regard for comprehensive planning and the interrelationships between modes. Trip-making by older people is complex, and all four transportation options must be considered in relation to one another. Depending on trip type and destination, the elderly person may walk to the grocery story, take the bus to downtown shopping, drive to the doctor, or take dial-a-ride to visit a friend. Most individuals have modal preferences, however, and commonly use only one transit type. Improvements of any one mode will benefit primarily a single class of user. A single mode incremental approach ignores the interrelationships between modes. Improvements should consider impacts on other modes so that total elderly mobility will increase as much as possible. A comprehensive planning approach insures that these considerations will be scrutinized.

References

Gillan, J., & Wachs, M. Lifestyles and transportation needs of the elderly in Los Angeles. *Transportation*, March 1976, *5*(1), 45–61.

Institute of Public Administration. *Transportation services of the elderly* (DHEW Publication No. OHD 76-20280). Washington, D.C.: U.S. Government Printing Office, November 1975.

Kemp, M. A. Some evidence of transit demand elasticities. *Transportation*, 1973, *2*(1), 25–52.

Kirby, R. F., Bhatt, K. U., Kemp, M. A., McGillivray, R. G., & Wohl, M. *Para-transit: Neglected options for urban mobility*. Washington, D.C.: Urban Institute, 1974.

Kraft, G., & Domencich, T. A. Free transit. Paper presented at the Transportation and Poverty Conference, American Academy of Arts and Sciences, Brookline, Mass., 1968.

Mullen, P. Estimating the demand for urban bus travel. *Transportation*, 1975, *4*(3), 231–252.

National Safety Council, *Accident facts*. Washington, D.C.: National Safety Council, 1967.

Paaswell, R. E., & Edelstein, P. A study of travel behavior of the elderly. *Transportation Planning and Technology*, 1976, *3*(3), 143–154.

Waddell, F. E. (Ed.) *The elderly consumer*. Columbia, Md.: The Human Ecology Center, Antioch College, 1976.

[1]This UCLA study of Southern California elderly discovered that 33 percent of the 65-year-olds and 51 percent of the 75-year-olds are immobile on a given day. These percentages reflect inadequacies of the transportation network, and are far higher than one would expect from illness.

[2]The out-of-vehicle time has been shown to be a critical determinant of senior bus use in many transit studies. A 15-minute wait at a bus stop is by far more critical than a two-hour bus ride (the in-vehicle time).

[3]Additional information about the trip survey can be found in the *Planning Handbook, Transportation Services for the Elderly* (The Institute of Public Administration, 1975).

[4]It is possible that some low-density surburban areas may be overserved by bus routing and frequency. Decreasing service and/or replacing the bus with a dial-a-ride might be the most appropriate response in these areas. Service to the elderly would be unaffected, and system savings through greater efficiency could provide additional service in other underserved areas.

[5]For information about specific vehicle improvements such as purchasing kneeling buses for handicapped/frail elderly access, consult the *Planning Handbook*, (op. cit.) IV 8–10 and IV 37–39.

[6]A 1976 Los Angeles study and a 1977 Buffalo study concluded that 80–85 percent of trips other than to the supermarket are made by automobile, either as drivers or as passengers.

[7]Dial-a-rides in Ann Arbor, Batavia, La Habra, and other cities with densities of seniors less than 2,000 per square mile have successful systems operating, open to the general population.

[8]Accident totals available only at a city level will not provide a sufficient profile of dangerous pedestrian environments. Appropriate neighborhood-level interventions require an intersection-by-intersection breakdown of pedestrian accidents.

[9]These considerations could include the timing and location of signaling or signing devices at intersections that are heavily utilized by older pedestrians.

[10]The formula of 4 feet per second for timing traffic signals is commonly used. According to this standard, a street that is 100 feet wide should require no more than 25 seconds to cross.

CRIME PATTERN ANALYSIS AND INTERVENTION TECHNIQUES

Nancy Ward,
Terry Watt,
and Victor Regnier

Nancy Ward is a Planning and Agency Rela-
tions Associate with United Way, Region IV,
Los Angeles County, Los Angeles, California.

Terry Watt is a Planner with EDAU Environ-
mental Planning and Landscape Architecture,
Newport Beach, California.

Victor Regnier is Associate Professor with a
joint appointment in the Department of Archi-
tecture and the Housing Research and Devel-
opment Program, University of Illinois at
Urbana-Champaign, Urbana, Illinois.

Introduction

Despite increased public awareness concerning the problem of crime against the elderly, progress in addressing this problem has been constrained by the limitations of victimization data. Although statistically persons 50 years of age and older have a lower rate of victimization than persons under 50, it is critical to recognize that the elderly are by far the most vulnerable members of our society in the aftermath of crime (U.S. Select Committee on Aging, 1977). Findings reported by the Midwest Research Institute Study of Kansas City, Missouri (1977) suggests that older people are less prepared to secure and protect themselves than their younger counterparts. The report also suggest that older persons suffer long term consequences of victimization because they are less resilient physically, economically, and psychologically. Signficant correlations have been found between the fear of crime and diminished elderly activity and increased isolation (Clemente & Kleiman, 1976). Thus, fear of crime may be more debilitating than actual victimization because of the limits it places on mobility.

Agencies providing services to the elderly can be instrumental in addressing this problem by instituting programs which lessen the older person's unfounded fear of crime as well as reducing rates of victimization. Effective intervention techniques should be tailored to the needs identified at a specific community or neighborhood level, since differences in neighborhood composition will affect the type of crime problem that may need to be addressed. Older people themselves can be a valuable community resource because they frequently spend time at home and can monitor neighborhood activity (Midwest Research Institute, 1977). Police services can be supplemented by encouraging this kind of neighborhood involvement and citizen awareness.

Improving the State of the Art

Since crime intervention programs must be tailored to the specific characteristics of the local crime problem, the planner should become familiar with the nature of the police department and its reporting system. Many departments have instituted crime prevention units or have placed emphasis on community resources for use in crime prevention. However, these programs rarely integrate data specific to the target neighborhood or the community for which they are planned.

Planners should be aware that problems often exist in the availability of data. Some police departments have adopted sophisticated data processing systems for documenting information about crime and victimization. However, unless the system is programmed to capture information about victims on an age-cohort basis, it will not provide information needed in planning for the elderly. Many smaller departments use hand calculating methods to tabulate crime data and do not keep separate accounts of victim characteristics (Maltz, 1972). Because information storage and retrieval capabilities vary, the planner will need to become familiar with local police records.[1]

Crime data are subject to a number of variations. The definitions of crime categories may vary, and this can cause distortion in the definition of elderly crime problems. Furthermore, crimes are classified by the seriousness of the incident. Thus, while a single incident may involve several crimes, only the most serious crime will be noted in police records.

Collecting recorded data. Data collection begins with an operational definition of the area to be studied. Crime prevention programs tend to be most effective at a neighborhood scale; therefore, it is helpful first to identify neighborhood boundaries. A check of local planning and land use agencies may reveal the existence of predetermined neighborhood designations. Once neighborhood boundaries are established, it is necessary to relate these to police reporting or patrol car districts.

In many instances police reporting districts will coincide with census tract or block group census boundaries. If this is the case, census data can be used to establish the elderly population of the area. Depending on the size of the target area selected, it may be necessary to examine census block statistics.[2] It is extremely important to identify the total number of elderly and non-elderly people in the target area in order to determine the rates of various crimes. Because the majority of offenders in cases involving elderly victims are juveniles, it also is important to identify the proportion of the population under 18.

If computerized victimization data is available it is possible to obtain data for the community or district scale. However, if data is gathered manually, it may be necessary to severely limit the size of the investigation. In either case it is wise to limit offenses to those categorized under the Part I classification of major crimes.[3] White collar crime such as fraud and bunco may be added, because a large number of older persons are affected by these crimes.

It is valuable to collect data covering at least two calendar years. A two-year time frame compensates for crime fluctuations. Trends in crime may vary with seasonal differences, school vacation periods, and holidays; such trends may influence prevention strategies. Where constraints preclude this data collection strategy, time sampling procedures can be used. Data can be collected using an interval time period of once per week, or a series of months can be intensely investigated. If an interval sampling procedure is used, the day of the week sampled should be randomly selected for each week. Police knowledgeables may provide advice about the most appropriate time sampling alternatives.

Once a target neighborhood has been defined, data gathering may proceed. The best source of data is the statistical information available from crime reports. Police reports include a great deal of incidental information about the criminal act. Salient information about the victim and offender must first be abstracted from the crime report before it can be analyzed. Figure 1 outlines salient variables that should be recorded. Transcription to color-coded index cards can facilitate sorting by neighborhood or monthly reporting period.

Problems with collecting recorded data. The three major constraints to data transcription include (1) confidentiality of records, (2) time limitations, and (3) inconsistent filing systems. Some police departments insist on keeping police reports confidential. In this case it may be possible to have police officers obtain needed information by recording salient portions of the police report. A joint effort of police and

Figure 1
Salient Victimization Data

REPORTING DISTRICT _____ DATE_____

TIME OF CRIME _____

TYPE OF CRIME_____

LOCATION: ADDRESS _____

SETTING _____

VICTIM: AGE_____   SEX_____   RACE_____

INJURY TO VICTIM? _____

_____

SUSPECT: AGE_____   SEX_____   RACE_____

OTHER _____

planner in gathering information from the records may be considered helpful to the police department and may provide the department with helpful information.

The amount of time spent on data collection depends on the accessibility of the files, the filing system utilized, the time period to be covered by the survey, and the number of crime categories scrutinized. Time-sampling crime reports or eliminating crime categories will reduce transcription time.

Police reports may be filed by date, reporting district, or crime type. If reports are filed by date, all of the files for the time period desired must be surveyed. If reporting districts are used for retrieval, a large number of irrelevant files may be eliminated from the survey. Similarly, if reports are filed by crime type, searching through many files will be unnecessary. The sampling strategy should be based on the filing system used by the department.

It is important to note that police reports do not present a complete or error-free picture of crime in the neighborhood; considerable crime remains unreported. Additionally, police data may be inconsistent because individual officers have variations in their reporting style. These differences may be reflected in the categorization of crime or the lack of detail about the physical setting of the crime. A common misleading practice is the filing of reports under the crime that was the most serious when multiple crimes occurred. For example, a robbery may be filed under aggravated assault if the victim is seriously hurt during the course of the robbery. Crime classification decisions are often made quite subjectively.

Contacting Police Knowledgeables

Should police statistics be unavailable, it may become necessary to contact the crime prevention unit of the police department. These police personnel usually have a comprehensive overview of crime and normally compile information on various aspects of crime. They can provide essential information on the history and development of crime prevention programs for the elderly. If there is no identifiable crime prevention unit in the police department, it may be necessary to contact the community relations officer for information about their crime prevention activities. Crime location pin maps maintained by the investigative division of the police department may prove helpful in specifying crime patterns; however, in most cases these maps will not be age specific.

Prioritizing target neighborhoods should be done in conjunction with policemen who are familiar with the city's various problem areas. Once specific areas have been defined, it is important to contact patrolmen who have frequently worked the area. The perceptions of these patrolmen about the nature of crime may prove invaluable. One technique for acquiring this information is to ask area patrolmen to document crime problems on a large-scale map of the neighborhood. Asking a patrolman to pinpoint trouble spots on a map can elicit information about locations and modes of crime as well as victim and offender characteristics. Specific questions should be included to determine what locations patrolmen perceive as areas of high elderly visibility and victimization. These officers may have valuable suggestions for the neighborhood.

Another technique to identify trouble spots in a neighborhood is a police "ride-along." Riding along with the police officers, the planner can pinpoint locations of high crime and can obtain insights into the physical and social nature of the neighborhood. The planner should use a map of the area to record salient locations of high crime and the associated physical characteristics of these areas. This technique allows the observer to note the physical layout and social composition of the community as well as police attitudes and behavior toward the elderly.

Contacting Community Organizations

Community organizations are a valuable resource base for information about crime prevention strategies and citizen concerns. Organizations may be local or part of a statewide or nationwide network. Police department officials or community service inventories may identify community organizations that participate in providing crime prevention services. These organizations may be best equipped to implement crime prevention programs for the elderly. Identifying these organizations provides the planner with a view of existing community supports. A comprehensive inventory can determine available existing services, needed new programs, and opportunities for coordination.

Conducting a Survey

If data are unavailable from crime reports, it may be necessary to survey the population. A survey can help to identify behavioral manifestations from fear of crime, awareness of special programs, criticisms of existing programs, security needs, and elderly perceptions of the problem. This kind of information can be helpful in developing new programs and evaluating ongoing programs. Figure 2 illustrates an instrument used in several cities throughout the United States to investigate problems of crime and the elderly. Survey approaches can be quite costly and time-consuming; therefore, they are not recommended unless the agency has considerable funding allocated for the analysis of this particular problem.

Figure 2
Crime Survey Model Instrument

SECTION I. BACKGROUND INFORMATION

Your answers to the questions in this survey will help us in providing ways to protect all senior citizens.

Since these questions deal with background items, you may feel that you do not want to answer some of them. However, this entire questionnaire is strictly anonymous. There is no way you can be identified, so we hope you are willing to give accurate information.

Your answers may be very important in helping us solve the special problems of you and your fellow senior citizens.

1. Please give your age: ___
2. Sex ___ Male   ___ Female
3. Living arrangements:
   ___ I live alone.
   ___ I live with 1 other person.
   ___ I live with 2 or more others.
4. Housing:
   ___ I own my own home.
   ___ I am renting my home.
   ___ I live with relatives.
   ___ Other.
5. Daily Activity:
   ___ I am self-sufficient for almost all routine household and shopping chores.
   ___ I have some help for these routine needs.
   ___ I have help for most of these needs.

SECTION II. GENERAL SURVEY

1. How often do you go out after dark?
   ___ 4 times a week or more
   ___ 1 to 3 times a week
   ___ 1 to 3 times a month
   ___ Less than once a month
   ___ Never
2. When do you feel safe in your home or apartment building?
   ___ Never   ___ Daytime
   ___ Nighttime   ___ Always
3. When do you feel safe in your yard or grounds of apartment?
   ___ Never   ___ Daytime
   ___ Nighttime   ___ Always
4. When do you feel safe in your neighborhood?
   ___ Never   ___ Daytime
   ___ Nighttime   ___ Always
5. When do you feel safe in the shopping areas you use?
   ___ Never   ___ Daytime
   ___ Nighttime   ___ Always
6. When do you feel safe on public transport?
   ___ Never   ___ Daytime
   ___ Nighttime   ___ Always
7. When do you feel safe in your car?
   ___ Never   ___ Daytime
   ___ Nighttime   ___ Always

8. Have you had contact with the police since living here?
   ___ No   ___ Yes, once   ___ Yes, twice
   ___ More than twice
   If you answered "No" to Question 8, go to Question 13.
9. If you said "Yes" to Question 8, what were the circumstances? Check *all* that apply:
   ___ I was the victim of a crime.
   ___ I was in an accident.
   ___ I was ill.
   ___ I needed other assistance.
   ___ Other. Explain: _____
   _____
10. If you answered Question 9, how would you describe the response time of the police?
    ___ Excellent   ___ Average   ___ Poor
11. If you answered Question 9, how would you describe the overall service provided by the police?
    ___ Excellent   ___ Average   ___ Poor
12. If you answered Question 9, how would you describe the overall service provided by other agencies involved?
    ___ Excellent   ___ Average   ___ Poor
    ___ What other agencies were involved?
    _____
    ___ No other agencies were involved
13. Have you ever attended a program presented by the police department?
    ___ Yes   ___ No
14. What was the subject discussed? _____
    _____
    ___ I do not remember.
15. Have you adopted crime prevention techniques as a result of the presentation?
    ___ Yes   ___ No
16. If you *have not* had personal experience, how would you describe the police protection in your neighborhood?
    ___ Excellent   ___ Average   ___ Poor
    ___ I have had personal experience with the police.
17. To what extent has your feeling about crime hampered your freedom of movement and activity throughout the city?
    ___ Greatly   ___ Somewhat   ___ None
18. If you were alone in your home and felt afraid, who would you call *first*?
    ___ Family   ___ Neighbor
    ___ Police   ___ Security Guard
    ___ Other. Explain: _____
19. Check each of the following things you usually do to protect yourself or your belongings:
    ___ Hold onto my purse or pocketbook and don't put it down.
    ___ Hide money in my home.

___ Hide money on my person.
___ Don't carry wallet or pocketbook.
___ Carry only minimum amount of money necessary for purpose of my trip.
___ Avoid going out at night.
___ Avoid certain streets and areas.
___ Go out with others, not alone.
___ Avoid using public transportation.
___ Have at home a lethal weapon (Gun, knife, etc.).
___ Have at home a nonlethal weapon (Mace, alarm, etc.).
___ Carry a lethal weapon.
___ Carry a nonlethal weapon.
___ Use special locks on my doors.
___ Use special locks on my windows.
___ Leave lights on.
___ Use timer to switch lights on/off.
___ Have my Social Security check mailed directly to bank.
___ Other. Explain: _____
___ None of the above.

SECTION III. VICTIMIZATION

1. How many times in the past 2 years have you been the victim of an offense?
   __ None __ 1 __ 2 __ 3 __ More than 3

2. What kind(s) of offense(s) were they? (Check *all* that apply and circle the appropriate number of times for each.)

What kind?	How Many?
___ Disturbing the peace	1 2 3 More
___ Assault	1 2 3 More
___ Purse Snatch/Pickpocket	1 2 3 More
___ Theft of property	1 2 3 More
___ Rape	1 2 3 More
___ Fraud/Con Game	1 2 3 More
___ Property destruction	1 2 3 More
___ Theft from mailbox	1 2 3 More
___ Other. Explain: _____	

___ I have not been a victim.

3. Think of the one offense against you in the past 2 years you consider the most serious. (If none in past 2 years, choose the most serious since you were age 55.)
   I have chosen an offense:
   ___ Occurring in the past 2 years.
   ___ Occurring more than 2 years ago.
   ___ I have not been the victim of a crime since I reached age 55.
   (IF NONE, you are finished with this questionnaire. Thank you.)

4. Thinking of the *one most serious* offense, what kind of incident was it?
   ___ Disturbing the peace

___ Assault
___ Purse Snatch/Pickpocket
___ Theft of property
___ Rape
___ Fraud/Con Game
___ Destruction of property
___ Theft from mailbox
___ Other. Explain: _____

5. Was your home entered against your wishes?
   ___ Yes ___ No

6. Were you threatened with harm?
   ___ Yes ___ No

7. Were you attacked physically?
   ___ Yes ___ No

8. Did you lose any money or belongings?
   ___ Yes ___ No

9. If you said "Yes" to Question 7 or 8, how much dollar loss did you suffer, including what was taken or damaged, and your medical expenses?
   ___ Under $50   ___ $50 to $200
   ___ $200 to $1000   ___ Over $1000

10. Did you notify the police?
    ___ Yes ___ No

11. If you did not notify the police, why not?
    ___ I was too frightened.
    ___ I didn't think they would try to do anything.
    ___ I thought they wouldn't be able to do anything.
    ___ I didn't know what number to call.
    ___ Other. Explain: _____

12. What is the age group of the person or persons who committed the crime?
    ___ Child   ___ Teenage
    ___ Adult   ___ Don't know

13. What time of day did it happen?
    ___ Morning ___ Afternoon ___ Night

14. How long ago did it happen?
    ___ In the past twelve months
    ___ One to two years ago
    ___ Two to three years ago
    ___ Three to five years ago
    ___ Over five years ago

15. Where did it happen?
    ___ In my apartment
    ___ In my home
    ___ In my apartment building
    ___ In another building or house
    ___ In a public space in my neighborhood
    ___ In public elsewhere
    ___ Other. Explain: _____

Source: Reproduced from *The Police Chief Magazine*, February 1977 issue, with permission of the International Association of Chiefs of Police.

Data Analysis

Geographic Mapping. Once descriptive crime data have been collected, the first step in analyzing the data is to create a "pin map" which plots crime locations. Using color-coded pins, these maps depict the location of various types of crime. These maps can identify areas or territories that support high crime activity and indicate where specific types of crime are most likely to occur. The physical setting in which crime takes place often has an impact on the type and time of crime and the modus operandi of the perpetrator (Midwest Research Institute, 1977). Figure 3 illustrates a typical pin map. This map depicts residential burglary and robbery against the elderly for a quarterly reporting period.

Particular physical environments may be more conducive to crime, and thus an analysis of victimization opportunity areas may be a necessary step in researching materials for a comprehensive crime prevention program. If design configurations which are conducive to crime can be identified, then interventions such as training or increased patroling can be used to reduce victimization. Such physical determinants of crime also can be used in analyzing pin maps of local crime.

The following six environmentally related elements identified by Gardiner (1977) are believed to have crime generating potential:

1. Areas of the neighborhood where urban support systems such as circulation, parking, zoning, and through traffic do not support the dominant land use of the neighborhood. For example, a truck route or heavily traveled road which divides the neighborhood may bring in strangers.

2. Porosity, which is the presence of parking lots, vacant lots and open areas. These areas allow access to the neighborhood and easy escape for intruders. Residential areas with vacant lots or parking areas adjacent to commercial strips are considered porous.

3. The presence of crime generators that attract outsiders who are potential offenders. For example, schools, supermarkets, or undesirable retail outlets may attract strangers to the neighborhood. Recognition of the crime generating potential

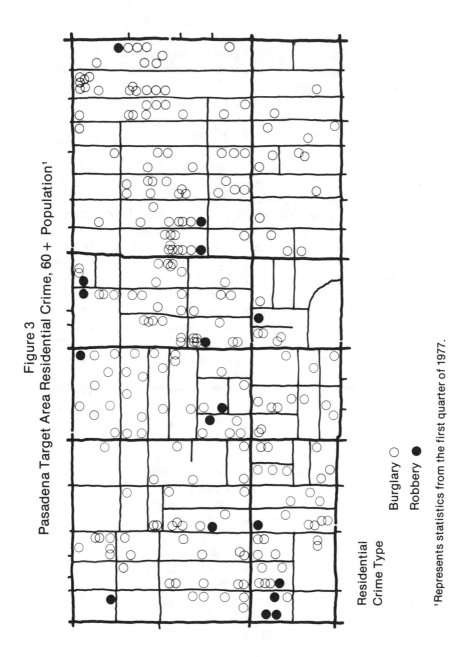

Figure 3

Pasadena Target Area Residential Crime, 60 + Population[1]

Residential
Crime Type

Burglary ○
Robbery ●

[1]Represents statistics from the first quarter of 1977.

of these services can lead to design modifications which create safer physical settings.

4. A neighborhood focal point claimed by outsiders. For example, a playground or park may become a gathering place or hangout for gangs.

5. A lack of clearly defined boundaries between districts or neighborhoods. When a neighborhood is clearly defined and residents are familiar with one another, outsiders are readily identified.

6. The lack of transitional zones between different types of land uses can lead to an inflow of potential offenders and can undermine community cohesiveness. For example, in areas where commercial activity is interspersed with residential use, potential offenders may go undetected.

Figure 4 provides an analysis of a typical neighborhood area which contains numerous opportunities for victimization according to Gardiner's criteria.

An analysis such as this can be helpful in prevention sessions with older neighborhood residents. The use of aerial photographs as a base map also facilitates visualization and neighborhood scale analysis. The comparison of actual crime locations with potentially hazardous crime settings can be useful in testing these criteria and locating particular sections of the neighborhood which can be targeted for intervention programs.

Descriptive Data Analysis

Recorded statistical data offer a variety of opportunities for analysis. Some of the most productive and enlightening analyses to be conducted are between victim characteristics and crime types. Crimes should be split into residential or street crimes and then further into categories that reflect harm to the victim. Victim characteristics, such as age, sex, race, type of injury, time of victimization, and whether or not the victim was alone can be helpful in understanding the problem. For example, residential burglaries or robberies that primarily occur during daylight hours may suggest a specific educational program orientation. This analysis will

Figure 4
Environmental Opportunities for Crime Against the Elderly

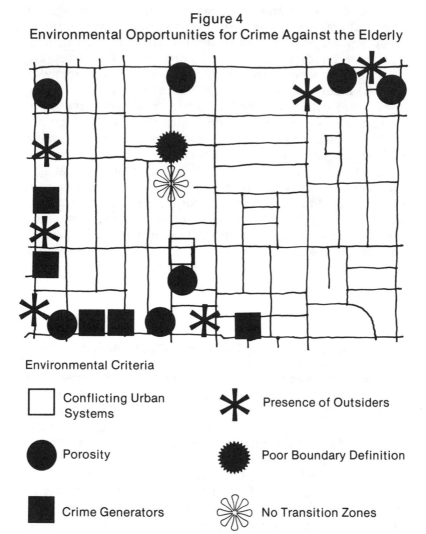

Environmental Criteria

□	Conflicting Urban Systems	✳	Presence of Outsiders
●	Porosity	✹	Poor Boundary Definition
■	Crime Generators	✾	No Transition Zones

produce information from which guidelines or prevention strategies can be written. Depending on the time and resources available, correlations between victim age and injury may be investigated, as these have specific implications for victim assistance programs.

Less obvious correlations, such as building type against suspect characteristics or type of crime, may provide insights about how the environment facilitates crime. For example, if apartment buildings with direct entry from the street are often robbed, then target-hardening[4] prevention methods such as double locking doors or loud alarm systems can be an effective deterrent. Because service planners rarely have the resources or expertise to deal with the source of crime, displacement of crime via preventative measures is the most realistic program possibility. Information gained through a crime analysis may provide useful information to social service agencies. These agencies may establish diversion programs directed to the groups responsible for criminal activity, such as recreation and job advocacy, which are commonly used to combat juvenile crime. Alternatively, these agencies may direct programs at the elderly to offer assistance, alter perceptions, or educate for crime prevention.

Implications

The significance of collected data lies in the implications they hold for crime prevention strategies. Because areas vary in their crime profiles, it is important to examine the total number of crimes in various categories to determine critical types of crimes. In some cases it is possible to judge the impact of certain crime types by calculating their portion of total crime. Additional information can be provided by analyzing patterns of criminal activity.

One successful crime resistance program in Wilmington, Delaware, used a series of related interventions in response to the fear of purse snatch and street robbery. Following an initial series of public meetings to arouse citizen awareness, the crime resistance programs were implemented. The first was a pocket-the-purse program handled by volunteers who spoke to various elderly women's groups. A sewing manufacturer developed patterns for internal pockets that could be sewn into summer and winter clothing. Volunteer seamstresses were recruited to help make and install the hidden pockets (Federal Bureau of Investigation, 1977).

Neighborhood block associations were encouraged to implement escort companion services for pedestrians as well as elderly ride-along programs. In addition, a program was developed to expand coordination with the police in handling truant school children.

Oftentimes solutions are initiated on the basis of supposition rather than good empirical data. In one city, plans were made to increase street lighting and improve transportation safety to the downtown area before it was discovered that the majority of crimes were occurring during daylight hours in the victim's own neighborhood. This again points out the need for developing accurate data in the early stages of any crime prevention project (Federal Bureau of Investigation, 1977). Collecting data on all crimes committed in the target area over a specified period of time will give a much clearer picture of the extent to which elderly are being victimized.

Statistical profiles can be useful in characterizing the general nature of crime, the type of setting, and the specific physical details important to that setting. Police reports will describe the percentage of residential burglaries involving forced entry and the percentage of unforced entries. A high percentage of unforced entries suggests the need for educational precautionary measures, whereas forced entry through louvered windows or single pin locks may suggest the replacement of door or window hardware. Formal adoption of a crime-prevention chapter of the local building code can be helpful, but may adversely affect low income individuals. Blanchard (1973) suggests a comprehensive array of issues that should be addressed in the development of a model security code. A primary concern is the differentiation of residential, commercial, and industrial building types with regard to emergency fire access. Typical contemporary security codes include hardware specifications such as dead bolt locks, window locks, and alarm systems as well as architectural guidelines suggesting the location of glass in doors, door construction, and the placement of unit entries with regard to street visibility. A physical survey of residential burglary sites could reveal characteristics of the apartment units or the setting which may suggest the form and substance of target-hardening programs.

Prevention activities should begin by stimulating public interest in the problems of crime in the community, particularly if there has been no previous organizational effort within the community. An excellent approach, effective in communities with dramatically rising crime rates, is the convening of a public meeting to air citizen concerns about crime. This can be followed by a demonstration or display of target-hardening devices.

Police departments can sponsor identification programs by loaning engraving devices to property owners to protect their belongings. Programs initiated to stimulate interest can effectively lead to larger neighborhood organizational efforts.

Intervention Techniques

Neighborhood watch organizations promoted by many police departments involve cooperation of neighborhood and building residents. The nature of the community may suggest the specific type of neighborhood watch program employed. A neighborhood composed largely of single family residences might be best served by small block associations of adjacent homeowners. Areas with large security apartment complexes are often more successful in instituting intra-building associations which acquaint residents and educate them about specific crime problems.

Once established, block associations can be maintained through a variety of organizational and motivational techniques. A critical element is the willingness of the police department to assist in leadership training programs and the establishment of mechanisms for maintaining contact between the department and the group (National Advisory Commission on Criminal Justice Standards and Goals, 1976).

Federal or city funds are often used to support block programs. Some cities provide matching funds to encourage and continue neighborhood block association activities. Community recognition of the worth of such programs is also necessary. This may take the form of annual awards recognizing outstanding coordinative efforts between citizens and police.

Neighborhood patrols. An additional tactic employed by some associations is the neighborhood or community patrol. This requires member volunteers to devote time each month patroling the neighborhood. Their presence on the street can be instrumental in deterring crime. In the West Philadelphia Community Walk program, volunteer groups, including seniors, are equipped with loud fog horns which arouse attention in the event of a problem. Walkers are instructed not to physically interfere with the crime but rather to sound the alarm and assist the victim. The West Philadelphia model uses the walking patrol to distribute crime prevention literature, to watch abandoned properties, and to visit the elderly and shut-ins (Washnis, 1976).

A further service which can be offered is the home security check. Volunteers trained by the police department survey homes upon request and determine where security improvements would be most effective. Various community service groups might be contacted to assist in financing and installing needed improvements, particularly for the elderly.

Victim assistance programs. Victim Assistance Teams (VAT) have been most active in dealing with the multiple problems of older victims. The principal responsibility of a VAT team is to provide mental and physical assurance to the victim. Program volunteers can also analyze the crime to help alleviate potential future problems. Most of these organizations provide immediate emergency service. In less serious cases coordinators review police reports involving older victims and follow up by delivering appropriate services. The actions taken by volunteers include making security checks, installing locks, assisting in the marking of valuables, and referring victims to social and health service agencies.

References

Blanchard, J. Proposal for a model residential building security code. In *Deterrence of Crime in and Around Residences.* Washington, D.C.: U.S. Department of Justice, 1973.

Clemente, F., & Kleiman, M. B. Fear of crime among the aged. *Gerontologist*, 1976, *16*(3), 207–210.

Federal Bureau of Investigation. *Crime resistance.* Washington, D.C.: U.S. Government Printing Office, 1977.

Gardiner, R. A. The environmental security planning process. Unpublished manuscript. Boston, Mass.: Gardiner & Associates, 1977.

Gross, P. J. Crime, safety and the senior citizen. *The Police Chief,* 1977, *44*(2).

Maltz, M. D. *Evaluation of crime control programs.* Washington, D.C.: Department of Justice, LEAA/NILECJ, 1972.

Midwest Research Institute. *Crimes against the aging: Patterns and prevention.* Kansas City, Mo., 1977.

National Advisory Commission on Criminal Justice Standards and Goals. *A call for action: Crime prevention and the citizen.* Washington, D.C.: U.S. Government Printing Office, 1976.

U.S. Select Committee on Aging, Subcommittee on Housing and Consumer Interests. *In search of security: A national perspective on elderly crime victimization.* Washington, D.C.: U.S. Government Printing Office, 1977.

Washnis, G. J. *Citizen involvement in crime prevention.* Lexington, Mass.: Lexington Books, 1976.

[1]A related problem concerns the definition and classification of crimes for inclusion in the FBI Uniform Crime Reports. All crimes are categorized according to the legal definitions of criminal acts. Residential robbery, for example, is distinguished from burglary by the fact that personal contact is made in the former case and not in the latter. Robbery is distinguished from larceny by the perpetrator's use of fear and force. The difference between petty and grand theft hinges on the value of the goods taken. The person involved in data collection should take care to develop full awareness of these distinctions, as they will be of considerable importance when it comes to deciding upon which programs will be most beneficial to institute.

[2]Chapter 2, *Secondary Data,* describes the availability of census block data.

[3]Part I crimes include the seven most serious crimes: criminal homicide, forcible rape, robbery, aggravated assault, burglary, larceny/theft, and motor vehicle theft. Motor vehicle theft was eliminated in this study and fraud and bunco were added.

[4]Target-hardening is the use of hardware such as locks or home security devices to make illegal entry more difficult.

AAA ROLE IN TRANSLATING TECHNIQUES TO INTERVENTIONS

Jay Glassman
and Michael Sneed

Jay Glassman is Director of Planning Development, Los Angeles County Area Agency on Aging, Los Angeles, California.

Michael Sneed is Head of the Research and Development Unit, Los Angeles County Area Agency on Aging, Los Angeles, California.

Introduction

Absence from the planning process of a clear and detailed understanding of local community support structures is a sin of omission as commonly recognized as it is continually committed. Contributing to commission of that sin are problems ranging from political and special interest group pressures to insufficient staff and time. In an attempt to cope with these problems and make better planning possible, the foregoing chapters have suggested and discussed data sources and techniques for data analysis which, while commonly missing from human services planning, are readily available and accessible throughout rural and urban areas of the country.

Network History

The national aging network, comprised of planners, administrators, service delivery professionals, and advocates, is a recent addition to the human service arena. Its formal inception came through the Older Americans Act of 1965, which established a system of Area Agencies on Aging (AAA) during the early 1970's to provide local planning bodies, advocacy, and comprehensive services for older person (60+ years). In order to carry out this charge and to develop coordinated systems of social services for the aged, the more than 600 AAA's engage in an extensive planning effort to direct coordination of resources, allocation of resources, and management of subcontracted funds to local communities.

AAA Role

The initial priority of the AAA's was to establish their role as organizations with local policy and planning responsibilities—a role recognized by the elderly, by other human service agencies, and by local political bodies. Having achieved that goal and accomplished many other organizational tasks, the priority has shifted. Currently, the emphasis is on use of the AAA administrative structure to develop and implement more effective, appropriate interventions in local communities.

In creating a system of more appropriate interventions, the AAA's have opportunities to avoid some of the past weaknesses of human services planning which resulted from a vague understanding of local communities. The aging network is relatively young and pliable and not yet afflicted with rigid predetermined programs, policies, or operations. Much of current human services planning suffers from this rigidity called elsewhere "dynamic conservatism," or the tendency of individuals to aggressively resist organizational change (Schon, 1971). Beyond early action to avoid dynamic conservatism, there must be attention paid to the array of problems which cloud clear understanding of local community structures basic to good planning. The most significant limit on effective planning is the constant realization that available resources directed toward the planning effort are insufficient. The looming deadlines and inadequate staff make any time-consuming or labor-intensive techniques of data collection and analysis unrealistic.

The creation of a data base for planning utilizing the time intensive processes of periodic, detailed, and direct surveys of older persons is clearly beyond the planning resources of the AAA's. AAA planners have traditionally responded to the planning data analysis dilemma by retreating from primary, direct sources of information and in their place have used a hodgepodge of other data sources because they are available, mandated, or intuitively understood to be useful. On rare occasions the intuitively chosen alternatives have proven successful, but successes remain rare.

The array of data sources which are commonly used by aging network planners includes the following (Harootyan, 1978):

    Public hearings
    Service provider input
    Information and referral data
    Informal sampling of consumers
    Advisory councils
    Secondary sources
    Direct surveys

Occasionally other planning bodies may be tapped for the results of their own direct surveys, but in the rare instances where that occurs aging planners are further hampered by the need to translate the results.

While the compromise—to use alternative sources of data—may fail to provide direct data from local communities, it can be a productive and positive compromise. Alternative data sources can provide a good picture of the local community if obtained, understood, and used with skill. Given both the dangers (invalid or inappropriate data) and the benefits (ease of acquisition) inherent in the compromise, planners must recognize the need to answer these questions:

1. What are realistic methods of data collection and analysis?
2. What are the pertinent data that should be collected?
3. How can the data be used to make decisions on the most appropriate interventions?

These questions can help to avoid the dangers of compromising a data source.

Review of Current Practices

The current array of planning practices are broadly characterized and some of the problems of data sources now used are demonstrated in the paragraphs following.

Most AAA's tabulate and to some extent analyze the demographic characteristics of the population eligible for service when creating their planning data base. This analysis, however, is rarely sufficiently sophisticated to allow the identification of population characteristics for smaller neighborhood areas. The other most prevalent practice currently employed in constructing a data base is a listing of formal service providers. A systematic analysis of the service inventory with regard to population characteristics is rarely made. A common failure is the complete disregard for the informal supports of a local community.

Local community service interventions are largely influenced by legislative mandates from a national perspective. On occasion local consumer surveys may play a role in determining interventions, but when that occurs, the validity of those consumer surveys is often called into question.

The most common determinant of the form and amount of service provided to a local community is the competition among local service providers for limited resources. While the basis of that competition may be the merit of the provider's proposal, the extent to which *merit* determines the outcome (rather than competitive skills) is difficult to determine. The allocation of resources is often based on nothing more than per capita share, with no clear or consistent weighing of that per capita formula.

In the AAA the use of secondary indicators is limited to easily acquired data. Often a particular secondary indicator may be used extensively only because it is well known. The easier a source is to access and manipulate the more useful and valid that source will be as an indicator of a community's support structure.

Conceptual Areas for Data Acquisition

While AAA's strive for ideal direct knowledge of a local community's dynamics, that ideal can only be achieved with a massive investment which is clearly unjustified in light of the critical need for direct services. We must begin now to overtly acknowledge our reliance on innovative and secondary indicators. A broad range of conceptual areas which are currently treated in a piecemeal fashion in aging planning are reviewed in this manuscript. Crime, land use, social services, secondary data sources, history, and transportation are all potential planning topics AAA's should have some information and control over. The following examines implications for the aging network in view of the AAA planners' need for better community data sources and analysis techniques.

Land use. Information detailing the physical characteristics of local communities is rarely used in planning supports for older persons in local communities. Physical planners are notably absent from the AAA planning process. Social planners, with undeveloped backgrounds in land use planning, are usually unaware of the possibilities of physical planning tools.

A seemingly obvious fact, often ignored, is that support structures cannot be effective if recipients are denied physical access to them. Various land use analysis techniques can facilitate the design of more effective services and of methods for evaluating how well consumers access those services.

Land use analysis can also give the planner critical information about a local community's physical terrain. Without that information, service planning may well result in service locations which conflict with other land uses. Land use analysis can reveal to service planners how physical characteristics can act as barriers or facilitators to service utilization. One innovative example is the use of inexpensive aerial photos which may provide significant insight about the residential neighborhood for which service interventions are planned.

Historical data. Specifications for the AAA mandated planning role in local communities are concentrated in a description of output rather than in the process for achieving that output. Yet a planner must have some appreciation for a community's history. While some aging network planners have worked in a particular city for years, many others, because the AAA system is newly established, are basically unfamiliar with that community's history. There is now no systematic requirement to develop a historical perspective of a planning service area. Closest to such an approach is the history commonly required of applicant agencies in the open, competitive Request for Proposal (RFP) process. Obviously that history is a very narrow and specific perspective on the local community.

While historical analysis may be informative, it should be considered as sensitizing and not directly suggestive of specific solutions to support problems. We need not repeat the mistakes of history. Historical perspectives can also reveal traditional ways a community copes or doesn't cope with problems—as, for example, in answering the question, "Has mass transit or the private auto been effectively used in the past to meet transportation needs?" With some reservations, a community's past performance can be used to project that community's future development.

Crime. The aging network has not allied itself with law enforcement agencies to any extent. Neither is the network mandated to develop programs relating to crimes against the elderly. However, there is an increased and mandated emphasis on programs for preventing dependence of isolated frail elderly persons. With this mandate there is increased awareness of crime as one of the major factors contributing to isolation, which in turn often leads to early and inappropriate institutionalization. At best aging network planning is a response to a general awareness that actual crime and perceived crime against the elderly may not be congruent but may have equal force in isolating older persons. More often crime programs are developed in an effort to secure funding rather than as a response to a local community need.

AAA's can structure alliances with law enforcement agencies when both agencies understand that they share mutual goals and objectives. Being able to ask the right questions can go far in cementing an alliance between the aging network and law enforcement. The techniques presented here can allow service planners to ask the questions which are both appropriate to their needs and to the way the law enforcement system is structured.

Transportation. Transportation has been mandated as a national priority for the aging network. It is also given central importance because it facilitates access to other critical support services.

Despite transportation's obvious importance, there has been surprisingly little carryover of general transportation planning techniques into the aging network. The transfer which has occurred is largely limited to vehicle design features. Current transportation planning in the aging network is particularly weak with regard to the specification of appropriate transportation interventions. AAA's do not collect or analyze information on transportation patterns of local communities. A listing of general population characteristics and existing transportation resources is normally the only transportation data base collected.

Techniques such as trip surveys can help to understand actual local transportation use patterns and identify the transportation gaps in those use patterns. Demonstrating the importance of pedestrianism and identifying obvious physical barriers to pedestrian flow are issues rarely tackled by service planners. The identification of underutilized transit system routes as well as overutilized routes can serve as a beginning in assessing the system's performance. The identification of transit dependents matched against characteristics of the transportation system is a useful process currently missing from the efforts of service planners.

Secondary data analysis. The AAA's have largely relied on secondary data from the U.S. Census. Secondary data can be immensely useful particularly because it is easy to acquire and ubiquitous in nature. Census data, however, offers a perspective which is skewed to some degree from the needs of the aging network since it was not collected for the network's specific purposes. Other problems associated with the use of secondary data can be related, but the most obvious is the lack of currency (as with U.S. Census done in 1969). Because of its obvious benefits, secondary data is used by the aging network as a basic determinant in resource allocation and in planning coordination of resources. The current state of the art is to allocate resources to local communities on a simple per capita basis without knowledge of how special populations in target areas will be served.

A needed refinement in the present use of secondary data is the addition of other sources besides the U.S. Census, such as Social Security records of older persons who are recipients of Supplemental Security and Medicaid benefits. Another refinement in secondary data sources would be the use of more sophisticated methods of analyzing the data. Accessing computer tapes of U.S. Census data to make those aggregations more specific to aging population needs as well as techniques for projecting population distribution from Census data should be investigated.

Service inventory. As one of the two informational elements commonly used in the AAA's mandated planning role (the other being population characteristics), lists of service providers are ritualistically provided as a preliminary part of the planning effort. The common practice of listing service resources gives no insight into the impact of those services on the older population. Lacking any quantitative measure of the services, it is impossible to determine the relationships between services available and population characteristics in order to establish gaps in service provision.

Current AAA planning rarely addresses the question of gaps. At best, there is identification of the number of older persons and an assumption of their need for services. A common example of current practice's "best" is to go one step beyond simple alphabetized lists of resources and index them by categories. Little or no consideration is given to informal support resources of the community—a failure which is increasingly less excusable in view of the findings from the U.S. Government Accounting Office Study in Cleveland which indicate that the frail older person receives 80 percent of his or her support from the informal system.

Given the techniques for soliciting relevant information on services, AAA planning could be made more effective through quantification of each service. Knowing that a certain number of homemaker hours were available to the community rather than just "some" homemaker services is an obvious example of the first step to identifying and quantifying service gaps in the local community and towards identifying the "best" intervention for in-home supports.

Implications

Given better techniques for gathering and analyzing data from local communities, the aging network can realize three major benefits:

1. Aging services policy making can become a more rational process.
2. The role of AAA's in delivering broad guidelines and technical assistance to local communities can be specifically defined.
3. Local communities can participate in planning and decisions about local service interventions in a more meaningful way through increased, specific expertise.

Toward a More Rational Policy

Policy decisions from the national level to those governing day-to-day decisions are responses to multiple social and political pressures rather than a consistent technical process based on sound information. While the political process gives some picture of social needs, it unquestionably distorts in favor of the most politically adept groups. It is unlikely and grandiose to suggest that any technical process for drawing a clear picture of social need could eliminate that political process. It is not unreasonable, though, to suggest that such techniques could help us understand the distortions introduced by the political process and thereby move toward more rational policymaking and more effective service provision.

AAA's, standing at the last step before direct service delivery, have been faced with a mandated role that has been defined only partially. Within a broad planning mandate there has been no clear distinction between planning responsibilities at various levels of the aging network. Certainly the local communities have a planning responsibility, but how might that responsibility overlap with the AAA? How broad or how specific should be the planning of the AAA as it relates to local community on one hand and to the State Unit on Aging on the other? The questions continue through all levels of the network, and are pragmatically answered, with variations, throughout the network. Given a consistent method for creating a picture of social need from the local community and aggregated throughout the entire network, it will become possible to identify network roles by specific activities, tasks, and outputs.

With that, we can begin to develop more specific definitions of roles and relationships between local community service areas and their service providers. The AAA in its planning for services at a local community scale must share a clearer relationship with the State Unit and the Administration on Aging, both of which are several levels removed from specific local decisionmaking. How will the AAA define local community service sites in planning and service areas? What better ways of identifying focal point agencies exist, other than the competitive process? How specific should the AAA's planning involvement be with local communities? How is that level of specificity attained? What techniques are relevant to the AAA for its own use in understanding the planning area, and what techniques should it expect of local community agencies? What kind of aggregated information should state units expect from each AAA? These are some important questions which must be addressed.

Local Community Involvement

Bringing decisionmaking to the local community level has been an important goal in recent years. It is difficult to assess if decisionmaking has indeed shifted to local communities in a significant way, or if in fact it has shifted away. Providing local communities with the techniques to assess and substantiate their own unique social needs and then institutionalizing the use of those techniques can do much in giving those local communities a significant voice in decisions about their service interventions. Through developing the techniques for creating an accurate picture of local support structures we can achieve a level of specificity regarding assessment of social need and type and amount of resources required for that identified social need below which federal, state, and AAA's need not and will not go. Given consistent techniques, local communities would be identified as the ultimate decisionmakers in their own unique programs within general mandates of resource allocation to the broader society and in conformity to generally accepted levels of quality.

References

Schon, R. A. *Beyond the stable state.* New York: Random House, 1971.

Harootyan, R. *Study of methods used by Area Agencies on Aging to access needs of older persons* (report). Sacramento, Calif.: California Department of Aging, October 1978.